Political Authority and Bureaucratic Power

Political Authority and Bureaucratic Power

A Comparative Analysis

EDWARD C. PAGE
Lecturer in Politics
University of Hull

The University of Tennessee Press
Knoxville

First Edition

Published in the United States of America in 1985 by
The University of Tennessee Press, Knoxville 37996-0325

Library of Congress Cataloging in Publication Data

Page, Edward C.
  Political authority and bureaucratic power.
  Bibliography: p.
  1. Bureaucracy.   2. Authority.   3. Leadership.
  4. Comparative government.   5. Weber, Max, 1864–1920.
  I. Title
  JF1501.P34   1985   350′.001   84-21895

  ISBN 0-87049-545-6

Printed in Great Britain

Contents

Acknowledgements   vii

1. Introduction   1
   What is bureaucracy?   6
   The plan of the book   12
2. The Job of the Official   14
   Career bureaucracies?   15
   Specialisation and training   25
   The role of officials   30
   Conclusion   33
3. Competences and Hierarchy   35
   The division of competences   38
   Hierarchy and top-down policy-making   43
   Territorial differentiation, functions and hierarchy   48
   Conclusion   63
4. Parliament in a Bureaucracy   65
   Legislation: a negative power?   68
   Budgetary control   73
   Legislative scrutiny   79
   Parliament as a training ground for political
      leadership   85
   Conclusion   89
5. Interest Groups and Bureaucracy   91
   Issue networks in the United States   94
   Pressured-group politics in France   98
   Rule by interest groups in Germany?   100
   Interest-group consultation in Britain   103
   Conclusion   105
6. Collegiality, Advice and Courts   107
   Cabinets and collegial decision-making   109

Advisers and ministers' personal staffs 115
Courts and judicial review 121
Conclusion 128
7. The Scope for Political Leadership 131
The role for comparative analysis 132
The concept of political leadership 135
Constraints on political leadership 139
Cross-national variations in constraints on
  political leadership 141
France: a problem of supply? 147
Leaderless democracy in the United States 150
West Germany: the reaction to the strong state 153
Britain: a particular problem of supply 155
Conclusion 160
8. Political Authority in Bureaucratic Systems 162

Bibliography 173
Index 189

Acknowledgements

Dr Michael Hawkins of Kingston Polytechnic originally suggested that Weber's work on bureaucracy could be used as a means of analysing contemporary political systems in a comparative perspective. Professor Jack Hayward offered encouragement and advice while I was writing this book, and, with two other colleagues at Hull University, Dr Philip Norton and Dr Noel O'Sullivan, offered valuable comments on an earlier draft of this book. The draft manuscript also benefited greatly from the comments of Professor Michael Goldsmith of Salford University, Thomas Mackie of Strathclyde University and Professor B. Guy Peters of Pittsburgh University. I am most grateful to these people for their help.

1 Introduction

In 1923 Rudolf Hilferding, the famous socialist economist and a left-wing Social Democrat, became the German Weimar Republic's sixth finance minister. His own civil servants were highly suspicious of him and decided that they would run the ministry without him. Nothing of any significance passed across his desk. Their action led directly to his nervous breakdown. After he returned to work the collaboration of his officials was only guaranteed once he had agreed not to make any radical policy initiatives (Jacoby 1973: 163). Hilferding learned the hard way what most of us already know: that permanent officials have political power. This book is concerned with assessing the scope for political action by non-officials within a system in which officials have power.

The fact that we know and accept the proposition that permanent officials have political power highlights the importance of understanding the nature of the bureaucracy in the study of any political system. While other sets of actors in the political process, such as voters, legislatures, parties, the Cabinet and pressure groups, are undoubtedly important in understanding why governments pursue particular policies, the role of the administrative staff is particularly crucial. It is the body actually entrusted with carrying out decisions and thus has a particular importance in policy-making in any political system. As Weber (1972: 126) wrote, *Herrschaft ist im Alltag primär: Verwaltung* ('everyday rule is primarily administration'); the administrative apparatus actually operates the machinery of government, and the degree to which these other bodies influence policy-making depends to a large extent upon the influence that they exert directly or indirectly upon the administrative system. Consequently, an understanding of the actions and dispositions of the administrative staff who exercise everyday rule, and of how they are influenced by groups and individuals from outside the civil service, is crucial in assessing the importance of these other sets of actors in the political process.

Furthermore, it is especially important that bureaucracy be assessed in a comparative context. A number of writers, from Hegel onwards, have pointed out that there is some form of developmental trend towards what may be termed bureaucratic government. Without necessarily assuming the existence of a Golden Age at some time in the past, a number of writers, beginning at least with Weber, have pointed out that this developmental trend poses problems which are similar for all polities; that increasing bureaucratisation diminishes the chances for the exercise of democratic public control of government. Such a view underlies Weber's discussion of bureaucracy as a general feature of the 'demystification of the world' (*Entzauberung der Welt*; cf. Weber 1972: 308) which leads to a potential weakening of the power of the publicly accountable politician. It can be found in Wolin's (1961) discussion of the 'age of organization and the sublimation of politics' in which he points to the decline in public authority resulting from the transformation of the public sector into 'an arena of diplomacy and negotiation for the new organizational statesmen' with the result that 'political society, in its *general* sense, has disappeared' (see also, Wolin 1981). Jacoby (1973) discusses the 'bureaucratisation of the world' and the threat that this poses for 'democracy', and Beer (1977) points out that the 'professional–bureaucratic complex' that emerges from welfare state development in the United States suggests a 'weakness of political actors to function as a national public'.

However, the developmental trends are usually either described at a relatively high level of generality or they are discussed within the context of a single country alone. In order to understand whether the particular features of the relationship between bureaucrats and politicians in one country are part of a general trend found among all bureaucracies or whether these features are specific to that country, we need a comparative analysis of bureaucracy.

But what sort of framework can be used to compare bureaucratic systems? One possible approach is to postulate something like a 'classical' distinction between politics and administration, or policy and implementation, and then proceed to show how this distinction cannot be maintained in the real world (see Putnam 1973). Thus officials, far from being the passive administrators described in the 'classical' model, merely carrying out the will of the elected politicians, are actually involved in policy-making: moreover, they know they are involved and actually enjoy being involved. The problem with such an approach is that it is doubtful whether many significant analyses of bureaucracy have ever been based upon the belief or assertion that this is the case, and thus it is hardly illuminating to reveal that such a classical model is inaccurate. Another method is to ask point-blank, 'Do the bureaucrats dominate the politicians?' There are several difficulties with posing the question in this way, not the least being that of interpreting what an answer to the question would mean. Would an affirmative answer mean that bureaucrats dominate all of the time, or just some of the time, and how much of the time would they have to dominate to be classed as dominating? A similar set of problems would accompany a negative answer.

In this book the question of the scope of political leadership within a bureaucratic political system is explored using an interpretation of an approach to bureaucracy offered by Max Weber (1864–1920), the German sociologist. Weber's most influential writing on bureaucracy was part of an unfinished work, *Wirtschaft und Gesellschaft* (Economy and Society), posthumously published in 1922 (here cited in its fifth edition, published in 1972). One must always be cautious when using Weber in discussions of bureaucracy for three main reasons.

First, the analysis of bureaucracy, like many other parts of Weber's approach, derives from a particular methodology of conducting sociological research, the 'ideal type' approach (for a concise discussion, see Giddens 1971: 141–4), which has given rise to much methodological debate. Therefore, to base an analysis of bureaucracy on concepts and ideas in Weber's work lays one open to the possible charge that one has misconstrued or misused this particular methodology.

Second, to seek to apply Weber's writing invariably means to offer some form of interpretation of it—another potentially hazardous exercise. Weber did not set up a single theory of bureaucracy. Rather, his work discussed what was specific about bureaucracy as a form of social and political organisation, the types of historical conditions that led to the emergence of bureaucratic government, the potential challenges that this poses for the exercise of political leadership, and the types of institution that could limit the potential for officials to dominate policy-making in a bureaucratic system. As Weber (1972: 572) states, the actual workings of a modern state cannot be simply deduced from the ideal-type characterisation. Instead, one has to apply ideal types, and the main guide to their application is to be found in the use made of them by Weber himself in his political essays (Weber 1958), and especially in his *Parlament und Regierung im Neugeordneten Deutschland* (*Parliament and Government in the Reconstructed Germany*) of 1918 and *Politik als Beruf* (*Politics as a Vocation*) of 1919, which refer to the conditions prevailing in Germany in the early years of this century.

Third, further interpretation of Weber's work in the field of bureaucracy risks adding to the devaluation through indiscriminate exposure of the thought of one of the most profound social theorists of modern times. Weber's approach has been much used in the past, often selectively (Mayntz 1965), through the borrowing and adapting of particular concepts found in his voluminous writings on the subject, or even as little more than a ritual bow in the direction of the acclaimed authority on bureaucracy.

If there are problems in applying a perspective suggested by Weberian analysis, why use one? There are two good reasons for potentially running the gauntlet of criticism from the field of political sociology as well as public administration in this way. First, while Weber did not leave us with a clearly-defined theory, tailor-made for cross-national comparison, he did leave us with a fairly comprehensive set of concepts and a particular method which could be used to analyse bureaucracy comparatively. Weber is, of course, not alone in this (cf. Riggs 1969, for example), but he does offer an elaborate set of concepts which are ambitious since they seek to explore the relationship between the institutions of public administration and more general questions about the nature of the state. As far as this author is aware, nobody has sought to use Weber's approach to do one of the jobs it was designed to do: to compare bureaucratic systems. Since the tools are there, it is certainly worth exploring whether they can be made to work. Second, the way in which Weber poses the problem of political leadership in a bureaucratic system is particularly attractive. Some have suggested that Weber saw the inevitability of administrators taking all important policy decisions (cf. Aberbach, Putnam and Rockman 1981: 1). Yet Weber explicitly rules out the inevitability of the dominance of officials (*Beamtenherrschaft*), which he treats fairly consistently as separate from his ideal-type construct of bureaucracy. In fact, he argued that there were features within his own society that appeared to run counter to the assumption that bureaucracy inevitably means the dominance of officials (Weber 1972: 572). For Weber the question of rule by politicians or officials was not an either/or one: he is quite clear that most of the activity of ruling is largely conducted by an administrative staff. Rather, he asks the question of what scope there is for political leadership within a bureaucratic system.

This book is not an essay about Weber's thought. It offers no criticisms of Weber's sociology, neither does it explore many of the wider but largely unrelated aspects of his sociological approach to politics that have made his work popular among students of issues such as social stratification and 'corporatism'. However, it is impossible to use his approach without offering some description of the basic framework, or rather this author's interpretation of it.

There are four key areas which have to be discussed: (a) what is bureaucracy? (b) how did it emerge? (c) what problems does it pose for modern democracies? and (d) what are the mechanisms that exist that can guarantee some form of political control over the administrative staff?

WHAT IS BUREAUCRACY?

There is no agreed definition of the term bureaucracy. One can trace its origins quite precisely to eighteenth-century France when it was coined by de Gournay (Albrow 1970: 16–17). However, this does not limit modern usage to any single meaning. There are at least four different sets of meanings of the term. First, there is the meaning which most closely resembles its semantic origins: bureaucracy as a system of rule. According to the more common variants of this definition, a bureaucracy is a governmental system in which officials dominate. The conceptualisation of bureaucracy as rule by officials to the virtual exclusion of all others is to be found in a variety of authors. Chief Justice Hewart (1929), for example, in his discussion of the *New Despotism* argued that the role that civil servants had adopted in the government of Britain, especially during the first world war had placed them at the pinnacle of a new form of bureaucratic government. From a different perspective, James Burnham (1962) argued that the development towards a system of rule by officials—a managerial society— was the inevitable development after capitalism. Burnham accepted the Marxian class analysis of society, yet he believed that Marx had failed to identify the crucial position of a new class of managers of both public and private organisations under capitalism, and that capitalism would develop to a state form in which this class of managers dominates. For Burnham, the Soviet experience was a clear example of this line of development (cf. Djilas 1957).

A second set of interpretations of the term bureaucracy sees it as a mode of conduct. This refers to conduct which is based upon the application of general rules. It is an interpretation that is found frequently in everyday language. When we say that a matter, be it a planning application or a complaint to a public official, is being dealt with 'bureaucratically', we mean that it will be processed according to a format defined by impersonal rules, taking the circumstances of the case into account only in so far as there are general rules to cover them. The term has also occurred in this usage in discussions of 'administrative discretion' in the social services: the idea that those responsible for social welfare benefits should have some discretion to ensure that there is 'just' treatment of the needy can be contrasted with the bureaucratic approach which argues that justice can only result from the impersonal application of general formulae, and that greater justice is achieved by improving the general formulae.

Thirdly, and related to this, there is a concept of bureaucracy as 'efficiency' or 'inefficiency'. In the sociology of organisations, as it developed in the 1950s and 1960s, Weber was interpreted (mistakenly; see Mayntz 1965) as suggesting that bureaucracy, as a system based upon formal rules and the other characteristics he discusses, resulted in greater efficiency in the performance of any organisational task. Most of the work of these analysts succeeded in demonstrating that the empirical link between efficiency and this conception of bureaucracy was rather tenuous. Yet it is still possible to find references to organisations regarded as efficient precisely because they were bureaucratic—the bureaucratic armies of Maurice of Nassau or Oliver Cromwell, or the water-management system in Ancient Egypt can be cited as examples of 'bureaucratic efficiency'. More commonly, bureaucracy evokes an image of inefficiency. By the nature of their activities, officials produce very little of tangible good to anybody else, and their work might appear to be simply red tape. As Herman Finer (1945: 110) commented in his review of some of the studies of bureaucracy in the 1940s, there is a common perception among them that 'the infirmities of public officials in the prosecution of their duties constitute the disease called bureaucracy. They are remediable, but not to the point of perfection.' Bureaucracy, according to this conception, is at best inefficiency, involving unnecessary rules and procedures, and at worst the stifling of all initiatives by using these rules and procedures actually to block them.

Fourthly, bureaucracy can refer to a social group—those who work in bureaus. This might apply to anybody who actually works in an office, whether public or private. More frequently, it is used to apply to office workers in public organisations, and especially to senior civil servants.

Doubtless, each of these ways of understanding the term can be read more or less easily into Weber's writing. However, the interpretation of his work used here regards bureaucracy as something more specific—an ideal type of social and political organisation. In offering this interpretation it is not intended to suggest that it constitutes the 'real' definition of bureaucracy, superior to all others. Albrow (1970: 124) warns that any attempt at a comprehensive definition is likely to be quixotic. Rather, it is the understanding on which the description and analysis in this book is based.

Bureaucratic rule (*Bürokratische Herrschaft*) is an ideal-typical form of rule which can be applied to non-state as well as state organisations, although here it will be discussed in the context of the state. The purpose of an ideal type was not to put forward a utopia, or even a preferred system of rule, neither was it intended to convey the 'average' or common characteristics of different systems of government. Rather, the ideal type was intended to present reality in a pure and abstract form so that the relationship between features of the abstracted ideal type could be examined and then applied to actual empirical experience to see how it deviates from the ideal type.

Weber distinguished between three main ideal types of rule: rational-legal (of which bureaucratic is the purest form), charismatic, and traditional rule. The difference between them resulted from the different claims that each system of rule has to legitimacy—the different bases on which citizens generally perceive an obligation to obey their rulers and on which rulers can claim obedience from citizens. Under traditional authority a ruler evoked the legitimacy of the 'holiness of ancient orders and powers, seemingly originating with time itself' (Weber 1972: 130), such as tribal or clan loyalities. Under charismatic authority, characteristically a rather unstable form, a ruler acquires his legitimacy through the personal possession of a set of characteristics judged to be exceptional within his society, as, for example, Napoleon I (see Weber 1972: 141). Rational-legal rule is based upon the acceptance of formal legal definitions of the powers of those placed in ruling positions, where the rights and obligations of both rulers and ruled are specified primarily through legal provisions.

A bureaucratic system of rule is a form of rational-legal rule which is based upon an administrative staff of officials. This is not to be confused with a system of government in which civil servants dominate, but rather a bureaucratic system is one in which government is carried out '*by means of* a bureaucratic administrative staff' (Weber 1972: 126). Of course, a great variety of governmental systems can be termed bureaucratic in this way. Monarchies, one-party states or liberal democracies, for example, can all be termed bureaucratic in so far as they rely upon a bureaucratic adminstrative staff, although, of course, the authority of the political heads of these bureaucratic systems is established through different principles. The administrative staff of officials has a number of characteristics which distinguish it from the administrative staffs of traditional and charismatic systems.

These characteristics can be broadly divided into three groups. First, the characteristics of the employment and career of the bureaucratic official: he is appointed on the basis of a legal contract, paid with a salary, has the post as a sole or main job, has a career prospect within the adminis-tration and has some form of technical training. Second, although not placed directly in his much-quoted list of ten characteristics of bureaucracy (Weber 1972: 126–7), Weber argued that a bureaucratic system is one in which officials have defined behavioural characteristics: the bureaucratic administrator must ultimately be compliant and must be prepared to administer rules dispassionately. It was this that he meant when he stated (Weber 1972: 563) that the bureaucratic system of government develops all the more as it 'dehumanises'. Third, the ideal type characterises the structure of the administrative staff. It is composed of a set of offices with clearly delineated responsibilities and operat-ing within a clear set of hierarchical relationships.

Over the extended purview of historical development which his wide-ranging analyses embrace, Weber notes a developmental trend towards a bureaucratic system of rule:

Just as the so-called progress towards capitalism since the middle ages is the unambiguous measure of the modernisation of the economy, so the development towards a civil service based on appointment, salary, pension, promotion, training and the division of labour, reliance on written procedures and hierarchical superior and subordinate relationships is the unambiguous measure of the modernisation of the state, the monarchical as well as the democratic. (1972: 825)

He outlines a number of factors that contributed towards the development of a bureaucratic system of rule in the modern state (Weber 1972: 556–71); the development of a money economy, the formation of large nation states, the extension of the role of the state away from defence and law and other towards economic and welfare concerns (see also Rose 1976a), the development of capitalism which placed demands upon the state to develop a form of organisation that allowed rapid and predictable state action, the concentration of financial resources in the central state, and the levelling of social and economic differences.

There are two main consequences of the ideal-type conception of the development of bureaucracy which are of interest here. First, since the bureaucratic system of rule is based upon the knowledge and the expertise of officials, there is the potential for the erosion of the power of the non-specialist who is placed in command of the bureaucratic administration. The head of the administrative organisation, whether a minister or a monarch, is a dilettante, and the trained civil servant an expert. Second, and related to this, as bureaucratic officials gain in influence, policy-making becomes transformed from a public into a more private and closed activity since 'bureaucratic administration is according to its nature always administration which excludes the public'. Further, civil servants themselves create secrecy: the 'concept of the official secret is manufactured by bureaucracy, and is defended with such fanaticism by it' (Weber 1972: 573). His conclusion is that the 'power position of a fully developed bureaucracy is always very strong and under normal conditions an overwhelming one' (Weber 1972: 572).

Weber discusses a variety of mechanisms which can limit the power of officials. In setting out the factors limiting the development of ideal types of rule, he (1972: 159ff) discusses three main limitations: legal norms which, especially in a rational-legal system of rule, may serve to limit the formal powers of public authorities; collegiality (of which Weber discusses a variety of forms) through which the monocratic principle which characterises the fully-developed bureaucratic system is diluted through the exercise of shared authority in a collective or collegial body; and the separation of powers involving legislative and judicial constraints on the exercise of executive authority. While these limitations are touched upon in his later empirical work, his analysis of Germany does not use them in a systematic way.

One of the more consistently emphasised potential limitations to the development of dominance by officials is the development of an effective parliament. The importance of parliament is twofold. First, public control can be partly exerted through the right to scrutinise the executive (*Enquêterecht*) (Weber 1972: 573), above all by the parliamentary right to gain access to specialised information. Second, public control can be exercised through the development of political leadership (see below), and parliament is the arena for the recruitment and training of the particular form of political leadership required to exert control over the bureaucracy. A further possible limitation, discussed in the context of business groups in the decision-making machinery of the German war economy, is the role of interest groups. Weber is somewhat ambivalent about whether interest groups actually limit the dominance of the official (see Chapter 5). Broadly, although he believed that extending to peacetime the wartime arrangements for the incorporation of business groups into the war economy would mean that the groups could dominate the state and its officials, he also argued that officials might develop close relationships with groups and utilise these relationships to gain greater expert knowledge and thus greater power.

Yet the most important of the limitations upon official dominance in a bureaucratic society discussed by Weber is the development of a particular group of political leaders who may be (but were not in Imperial Germany) appointed to head administrative organisations— professional politicians—which emerged alongside the development of bureaucracy (Weber 1958: 505). The professional politician is the 'representative of the political power constellation' (Weber 1958: 508) who can exercise leadership. The politician is a demagogue (which Weber uses in its classical sense, that is to say, largely stripped of its perjorative meaning), who struggles to build coalitions for the purpose of furthering his own political power and is held accountable for his actions. Weber equates the initiative of the politician with that of the capitalist entrepreneur, and contrasts it with the ultimately subordinate nature of the official. It was the absence of political leaders, or rather the exclusion of them by Bismarck, that led to rule by officials in Imperial Germany. The importance of political leaders in preventing official dominance adds to the importance of the political parties as well as parliament since they are the recruiting and training ground for the professional politician.

THE PLAN OF THE BOOK

This book asks three main questions. First, how far are the modern systems of administration in France, Germany, Britain and the United States bureaucratic in the ideal-typical sense discussed by Weber? Chapter 2 looks at how far the job of the administrator can be termed bureaucratic in the sense discussed by Weber: are the administrative systems staffed by career officials with specialist training who can be distinguished in their mode of behaviour from politicians? Chapter 3 explores the same question from the perspective of the structure of administrative organisations: can the bureaucratic systems of the four countries be characterised as a system of organisations with clearly delineated responsibilities and clear hierarchical relationships with other institutions?

The second question is Weber's own: what powers exist within a bureaucratic system to contain the potential for official dominance? This, of necessity, takes us well outside an analysis of the administrative apparatus alone. Chapter 4 explores the role of parliament as a means of exercising control over the administrative apparatus as well as its potential as a training ground for political leadership. Chapter 5 explores more closely the question of the degree to which interest-group activity serves to limit the exercise of authority by the executive in each of the four countries. Chapter 6 briefly explores the limitations on the power of officials through collegial forms of decision-making, through the use of advisers and personal staffs by the politician to counter the expertise of permanent officials. It also considers the role of the judiciary in applying the legal norms which, almost by definition, limit the competences of executive authority in a bureaucratic system.

The third question is: what is the scope for the particular form of political leadership that Weber identified as crucial in limiting the power of officials in each of the four countries (Chapter 7)? Finally, Chapter 8 discusses the value of the Weberian framework for the comparative study of public administration.

2   The Job of the Official

How closely does the actual job of being a civil servant conform to the Weberian ideal type of official? Given the historical conditions for the development of an ideal type of bureaucracy discussed in Chapter 1, one might expect a relatively high degree of convergence among bureaucratic systems in terms of their conformity with an ideal type: each of the four countries has a money economy; each country is large, with Britain's 56 million, Germany's 62 million, France's 55 million and the United States' 220 million populations. The state now undertakes a variety of functions which have extended very rapidly in the twentieth century to embrace a variety of costly (in terms of both money and manpower) social welfare functions, in addition to the more traditional functions of defence, tax collection and road building (Rose 1976a). Public employment in Britain now accounts for 31.7 per cent of the working population, in France 29.1 per cent, in Germany 25.8 per cent, and in the United States 18.8 per cent (Rose forthcoming). The state, whether in the form of central or decentralised units of government, has concentrated the power of revenue-raising in itself, with farming out tax collection a thing of the past (Barker 1944). There has been at least some democratisa- tion of public life and some levelling of social inequalities, not simply through the development of the welfare state (although it is possible to argue that inequalities are exacerbated by the structure of the welfare state; see Le Grand 1982) but also through increased social mobility and the decline in the importance of inheritance for future life-chances.

These broad historical trends certainly make for similarity

between the bureaucratic systems of the four countries as compared with the societies, ranging from Ancient Egypt and the Byzantine Empire to European feudalism, covered in Weber's encyclopaedic analysis. Yet we know that the conditions of appointment, the mode of recruitment, and the means of training and promoting civil servants differ markedly from one country to another. To find divergence between the ideal type and empirical reality on the basis of the contemporary administrative systems of the four countries is to be expected since the careers of officials vary. To point out that officials in Germany, France, Britain and the United States work within organisations that have different structures, and different criteria for appointment and promotion is to state the obvious, rather than offer a significant criticism of Weber.

However, the question of how far and in what way the job of the official conforms to Weber's ideal type is not an idle one since, as mentioned in Chapter 1, it is the nature of the job of the official, its permanence and the degree of specialist knowledge involved in it, that imposes one of the major constraints upon political leadership. By describing the nature of the official's job one is describing the type of people with whom politicians interact, and exploring whether they pose the sort of limitation to effective political leadership that Weber identified within a bureaucratic system.

CAREER BUREAUCRACIES?

A career bureaucracy refers to the existence of a 'system of regularised promotion' (Ridley 1983: 179), that is to say, an official can expect to make a career within the civil service and have the possibility of reaching the most senior positions within it. This would be contrasted with a system in which there is no regular possibility for internal promotion to higher administrative posts, with these posts being filled by those who have pursued careers outside the civil service.

The greatest contrast in terms of a career bureaucracy is that which emerges from the comparison between the civil services of the United States and Britain. The British civil service conforms closely to the Weberian ideal type; the United States has a career civil service alongside a non-career system, in which the higher levels of government organisations are staffed by 'political executives'; those who are nominated by the President or in the name of the President.

The American federal bureaucracy employs 2.7 million civilian employees of whom approximately 3800 may be termed political appointees (Heclo 1977: 38). There is a long tradition of the appointment of outsiders to the civil service which became especially associated with President Andrew Jackson's use of the 'spoils system' to reward political friends and helpers—offices at all levels of seniority were regarded as appropriate rewards for supporters. Indeed, the importance of this form of patronage was such that the 'whole structure of the mass Democratic Party of Jackson was firmly cemented by the award of federal offices, especially postmasterships' (Nelson 1982: 760). From the mid-nineteenth century onwards the system came under increasing attack, not only because it was a major target for corruption, with Nelson (1982) citing examples of newspaper advertisements offering government offices for sale for cash down and a percentage of wages, but also because it was perceived to produce incompetent government by people with no experience of public life.

The 1883 Pendleton Act was the main result of this attack. While its coverage was somewhat limited, it created the notion of a career service, with promotions on 'merit' (which frequently turned out to be simple seniority within the service) for a defined set of posts to be overseen by a Civil Service Commission. This did not put an end to the spoils system (see Nelson 1982) since the posts covered by the merit system could be amended by a presidential Executive Order. This led to the phenomenon of Presidents 'blanketing in' their nominees—appointing people to posts and then making them irremovable by converting the post into one covered by the merit system.

Over the post-war period there have been three major changes in the system of non-career appointments to the

American federal executive. First, political appointments have been concentrated in the more senior positions of the executive departments. Thus, using the mid-1970s data and personnel classifications (Heclo 1977: 38), 97 per cent of the Executive Schedule officials were political appointees, 23 per cent of the General Schedule super-grades were political appointees, and 0.06 per cent of the lower General Schedule grades were political appointees. Second, as Brown (1983) points out, political appointees have become less a reward to political friends and allies and more a matter of appointing those in whom Presidents have some reason to think they may trust or in whom they have confidence. Thirdly, and relatedly, the party itself has become less dominant in the appointment process and the White House has increased in its importance.

The American system thus has two paths to higher office within the executive departments and agencies: a career and a political path. In practice the two paths are not so neatly separable with, for example, career officials occasionally occupying posts equivalent to those held by political appointees in other agencies. The system is a muddle, as the senior aide to an ex-President quoted by Heclo (1977: 34–5) makes clear: 'The whole political-bureaucracy thing is all mixed up. I don't have a strong sense of where the line's drawn.'

Since the number of political appointees is likely to be large for any President, the appointment process is a complex one—far too complex to be conducted on the basis of the President nominating people known to him personally. A President usually relies heavily on a panel of evaluators in making the appointments. The posts open for political appointments are set out in the 'plum book' with who gets appointed the outcome of a 'social-political mêlée' in which different groups within Congress, the White House as well as interest groups and the agency or department heads already appointed seek to influence the outcome. In this system it is difficult to point to an overwhelming rationale for appointments, although under the Carter presidency there was a tendency to appoint people who were regarded as 'representatives' of certain interests (Polsby 1978) or, as

Heclo (1978: 112) put it, policy activists who had reputations as 'policy experts' in Washington. These policy 'experts within the various networks who are consulted' by those making appointments 'typically end by recommending each other'. Under the Reagan administration the appointments still appear to reflect some acknowledged expertise in the field, but display a clear preference for those who are likely to be more sympathetic to 'curbing big government' (Havermann 1981). In Heclo's (1983: 45) terms, the Reagan administration recruited from 'conservative networks of policy activists'.

On the career side, the recruitment to the career civil service was conducted by the agency or department itself with the collaboration of the Civil Service Commission, until it was abolished in 1978 with the setting-up of the Office of Personnel Management and the Merit System Protection Board. Under the old system, it was the agency or department which hired the civil servant, as long as the candidate had been certified to have suitable qualifications for the job by the Civil Service Commission. While the post-1978 system retains the principle of the department or agency as the main hiring body, the position has been confused by the creation of the Senior Executive Service which, it has been feared, gives political appointees greater scope for inserting career officials into particular agencies (cf. Lynn and Vaden 1979; Long 1981). Furthermore, the degree to which the jobs outside those in the 'plum book' are really career jobs is open to some doubt because there are a variety of means through which particular individuals can have their chances of getting a senior career appointment improved, such as through specifically designing job descriptions for the person one has in mind for the job (cf. Heclo 1977: 123–8, for a description of this and other methods).

In Britain, on the other hand, the traditional principle of recruitment to the higher levels of the civil service since the Northcote–Trevelyan reforms of the nineteenth century has been that of the inability of politicians to decide who occupies a senior post. Eligibility for promotions to the higher levels of the civil service, the three most senior ranks of Under-Secretary, Deputy Secretary and Permanent

Secretary, is contingent on the performance of the official in the more junior ranks up to Assistant Secretary. Both promotion within the lower ranks and promotion from the lower to the higher levels are largely in the hands of civil servants. Promotion within the lower levels is a matter for the permanent head of the department concerned, often in consultation with the minister for the relatively senior appointments. Eligibility for promotion into the higher ranks results from a successful interview with a promotion board composed of civil servants (cf. Ridley 1983, for a discussion of promotion in Britain and in a comparative perspective). For the most senior job of Permanent Secretary and Deputy Secretary the choice among those eligible is made by a complex pattern of consultation between the permanent head of the civil service, now located within the Management and Personnel Office, senior civil servants in other ministries, ministers, and the Prime Minister. The head of the civil service consults with other civil servants and sends out feelers about the acceptability of different candidates (see Treasury and Civil Service Committee 1982: 473). Ridley (1983: 188) summarises the subsequent procedures thus:

The head of the civil service then advises the prime minister who is responsible for appointments at this level, but, until the present [1979 Conservative] government, it has been a convention that this advice is followed. The process is harder to pin down as regards Permanent Secretary appointments. The head of the service makes suggestions to the prime minister on the basis of his own knowledge and consultations with the committees and ministers concerned.

The system of peer performance evaluation implied in this career path is somewhat short-circuited by the existence of a 'fast track' promotion career pattern. One of the criticisms that the Fulton Committee (1968) made of the British civil service was that it offered unjustifiably speedy promotion prospects for the academically educated, especially those with a degree from Oxford or Cambridge, through their appointment to the post of assistant principal, the lowest rank in what was then equivalent to the open structure. They were then earmarked for careful testing and scrutiny with a view to rapid promotion. The 'fast track' scheme, introduced in 1970, (the Administration Trainee scheme), according to which high-fliers enter the civil service, replicates many of the problems identified by Fulton— Oxford and Cambridge graduates made up 63 per cent of the direct entrants to the Administration Trainee scheme in 1981 (Civil Service Commission 1981), and the system of internal recruitment to the scheme from those already in the civil service has fallen short of expectations, with only 20 per cent of recruits to the scheme coming from within the service in 1981. Similarly, attempts made in 1981 to introduce a system to allow the rapid promotion of those within the civil service but not already in the 'fast track' scheme, the Higher Executive Officer (Development) scheme, has failed to produce any substantial results. In the whole of the first three years of its operation it only recruited twenty-five officers, in contrast with the thirty each year envisaged when the scheme was introduced (see *The Times*, 21 January 1984).

As Ridley's analysis shows, the traditional lack of direct involvement by ministers in the process has been altered somewhat by the Conservative Prime Minister, Mrs Thatcher. Mrs Thatcher has shown a more interventionist approach to top civil service appointments, especially in the case of Peter Middleton, an Under-Secretary in the Treasury, who was promoted, reputedly at her insistence, as of Spring 1983 to the post of Permanent Secretary at the Treasury ahead of others believed to be closer to the front of the line for promotion (see *The Economist*, 25 December 1982). Richard Crossman's diaries (1975: 119, 121, 230, 232) show that ministers have always expressed their views about who their Permanent Secretaries should be. However, the names of those in the running for a particular job are usually decided by civil servants. The minister's influence has traditionally depended on seeking to persuade the head of the civil service, maybe seeking to enlist the aid of the Prime Minister in the attempt to persuade. Mrs Thatcher's appointments have undoubtedly gone further than this. Yet at present it is not possible to equate the powers of the Prime Minister in Britain with the powers of the President in the United States. First, the power has been limited to new appointments, and secondly the power is still indirect by comparison with the existence of the 'plum book'; the listing of jobs over which the President has direct ability to make nominations. Furthermore, in the case of Middleton, it appeared to be his style as civil servant rather than his political leanings which endeared him to Mrs Thatcher. It was the same set of qualities which also endeared him to Denis Healey, a former Labour Chancellor of the Exchequer.

The British system can still be classified as almost purely a career system, the relatively greater intervention of some Prime Ministers notwithstanding. In France and Germany a pattern of merit appointments coexists with a system of political appointments, although the scope for political appointments in both these countries is far more limited than that found in the United States.

In France one major source of political appointments, or rather one major potential source, is the prerogative of the minister to nominate the *directeurs* (heads of division), the senior officials within his ministry. This right is, however, one which is circumscribed by a variety of factors: the possibility of opposition from Matignon (the Prime Minister's Office) or the Elysée (the President's Office) and the possibility of opposition from civil servants who object to the principle of an elected politician destroying the stability of the career structure of the higher civil service. As Suleiman (1974) points out, a minister is nevertheless able to replace a *directeur*, but this is a highly constrained power. In principle, a minister is able to appoint a non-civil servant as *directeur*, yet in practice the pressures from the civil servants themselves are sufficiently powerful to mean that a 'minister's choice . . . is, for all practical purposes, limited to the civil service' (Suleiman 1974: 142). Another route for political appointments is through the *cabinet*. This is an advisory staff of the minister which is intended to allow the minister greater control over his department by providing him with a specialist staff capable of keeping up with developments within the ministry as well as, in the case of the *directeur de cabinet*, being empowered to act in the name of the minister (see Chapter 6). In fact, the minister's choice is also effectively limited here; most members of the *cabinet* are civil servants. Furthermore, the system of *corps* (see below) limits the minister's choice of civil servants since certain *corps* have traditionally been represented in the *cabinet*, and to break the tradition means alienating these powerful groups within the French civil service. Although the ministerial *cabinets* have been a much admired feature of the French system, above all by the British Labour Party, it does not offer great possibilities for advisers from outside the service to help the minister take control of his ministry since almost all members of *cabinets* are civil servants. Over the past fifty years, 90 per cent of the personnel of *cabinets* have been civil servants, although this was lower in the 1981 Mitterrand government (Bodiguel 1983: 296).

Recruitment to the higher levels of the civil service in France conforms in outward form to the Weberian ideal type of career structure (for a discussion, see Salon 1980). Membership of one of the *Grands Corps de l'État* is one of the preconditions for access to higher posts in the French civil service, since they serve as the bodies from which senior positions are recruited, with particular posts frequently being regarded as the special domain of particular *corps*. Eligibility for high office in the French civil service is determined within the *corps* (cf. Thoenig 1973). For example, the *corps* of *Inspection des Finances* provides the senior positions within the finance ministry, and senior legal posts are usually staffed by members of the *corps* of the *Conseil d'État*. The *Grands Corps* include the technical *corps* of *Mines*, *Ponts et Chaussées*, *Armaments*, *Télécommunications* and *Génie Rural et des Eaux et Forêts* (see Halpern and Oury 1980). Access to the technical *Grands Corps* is through a system of special administrative schools, the technical *Grandes Écoles*, in particular the *École Polytechnique*, colloquially known as *l'X*.

For admission to the *École Polytechnique* a student has to sit a competitive examination (a *concours*) after studying for two years after the *baccalauréat* (the qualification required in France for university entrance) in a designated school which runs courses preparing students for the examination. At the end of the two years' training at the *École Polytechnique*, those who obtain the best grades at the final *concours* are offered posts in the *Grands Corps*, and this usually involves a further period of training at one of the many technical schools, such as the *École Nationale des Ponts et Chaussées* (see Salon 1980). Access to the non-technical *Grands Corps*, the *Conseil d'État*, *Inspection des Finances*, *Cour des Comptes* (see Escoube 1980) is primarily through the *École Nationale d'Administration* (ENA). After university study, candidates for the *concours* for entry into the ENA usually prepare for the examination at the Paris *Institut d'Études Politiques* (92 per cent prepared in this way in 1976). After the two years' study at ENA, performance is assessed through another competitive examination, with the best performers in the examination having the option of choosing the most prestigious *corps*. Indeed, it was the ability of technical and non-technical graduates of the prestigious *écoles* to choose their *corps* which gave the *Grands Corps* their title of *Grand*—a *Grand Corps* was one which the best students persistently sought to join (Escoube 1981: 28).

There are two other routes to the *Grandes Écoles*, through the second *concours* which enable those already within the civil service to take a specially designed examination for civil service candidates (although the second *concours* is frequently criticised for emphasising academic knowledge over practical experience), yet these form a relatively small part of the total intake of the *Grandes Écoles*. In 1983 the socialist government introduced an additional route to the *École Nationale d'Administration* through a *concours* designed specifically for trade unionists and those with local government experience (*Times Higher Education Supplement*, 19 August 1983).

The West German system of appointment offers apparently great scope for ministerial choice of higher civil servants, the so-called *politische Beamte* (political officials). The right of a minister to place a civil servant in temporary retirement with pay is enshrined in law (Article 36 of the *Bundesbeamtengesetz*). This usually affects the top posts of *Staatssekretär* and *Direktor*. Between 1969 and 1979, Seidentopf (1980: 237) states that 150 of the occupants of the top posts within the German federal administration were put on temporary retirement in this way, with 64 of the 150 going in the first two years of office of an incoming minister. Dyson (1977) points out that this apparent free hand is in practice limited by factors similar to those which limit the minister in France in choosing his *directeurs*—the pressures from the civil service itself. Dyson outlines the consultation that took place within the ministry when discussing new appointments through the system of the personnel councils (the *Personalräte*), advisory bodies composed of officials within the ministry, in the 1970s, and the importance of support within the ministry for the incumbents of senior posts. 'Where senior officials are appointed against the advice of the personnel council . . . internal support for that individual becomes problematic' (Dyson 1977: 7). This was especially noticeable in the case of Claus Noé, an appointee in the ministry of economics, whose difficulty in establishing authority within the ministry Dyson attributes to the hostility within the ministry surrounding his appointment.

As with the United States, to be within a career service is not to be immune from political influences, since the statistical evidence suggests that party membership is associated with career prospects even outside the legally-defined procedures used for creating *politische Beamte*. A study by Steinkemper in the 1960s (cf. Mayntz 1978: 200–1) showed that federal and state officials who were members of a party in government had a better chance of promotion than non-party members. Recruitment to the higher level of the civil service requires that one has entered the career path (the *Laufbahn*) of the higher civil service (the *höherer Dienst*; for a description of the different levels see Southern 1979). Entrance to the *höherer Dienst* requires completion of university study and success at the *Staatsexamen* (the state examination), which emphasises the legal and social sciences. The civil servant then has to be hired by a particular ministry for a probationary period, after which he takes a second *Staatsexamen*. The civil servant's promotion within the ministry is a matter for the ministry rather than a service-wide matter as in Britain—a principle eshrined in the German Basic Law (Article 65)—and frequently operates on the simple principle of seniority (Mayntz 1978: 167).

In the United States the numerical importance of political appointees at the senior posts within the executive makes the United States least resemble the ideal type of bureaucracy among the four countries. In France and Germany the legal power to appoint civil servants has not produced such a substantial body of officials at the head of the executive agencies who can be replaced—indeed expect to be replaced—when another party takes office. The constraints on a minister's choice in the appointment process are quite strong in both Germany and France. However, in both of these cases there is a substantial deviation from the ideal type. Of the four countries, the career structure of the civil service in Britain most closely approximates the ideal type.

SPECIALISATION AND TRAINING

Weber's analysis stressed specialist (*Fach*) training as a component of his ideal type of bureaucracy. Precisely what constitutes specialist training is, however, not clear. Traditionally studies have distinguished between 'generalists' and 'specialists' (Ridley 1968), with generalists being those who have a general education, usually arts-based, and specialists being trained in the 'hard', natural sciences, or the less 'hard' disciplines of economics or social sciences. However, if one takes specialist to mean that the training has a close bearing on the particular job of the official, then to state that some disciplines are more 'specialist' than others is to make assumptions about the nature of the job that officials, particularly senior officials, do. A senior official's job involves, for example, dealing with other departments, interest groups, parliament and ministers and not simply performing tasks demanding detailed knowledge of a particular scientific discipline. Thus, as Rose (1981) suggests, a background in classical Greek might be just as appropriate as a degree in physics, since this sort of activity is no less related to the Peleponesian Wars than it is to solid state physics.

The simple facts of the educational backgrounds of top civil servants in three of our four countries can be easily ascertained from Aberbach, Putnam and Rockman's (1981) study (see Table 2.1), the most striking feature of which is the importance of a university degree for high office, even among political appointees in the United States, in each of the three countries. It is the importance of university education, and the bias within the educational systems of each country in favour of high status social groups, which serves to make the higher civil service of each country socially unrepresentative—a theme taken up in many studies of 'representative bureaucracy'. (For an excellent review, see Sheriff 1976.) Such studies suggest that a civil service in a representative democracy might be expected to be sociologically representative of the nation as a whole. Of course, while the entire civil service taken together (that is,

Table 2.1: Educational background of top civil servants (%)

	Britain	Germany	United States CS[a]	United States PE[b]
No university	16	1	0	3
Law	3	66	18	28
Humanities (including history)	40	2	6	7
Social sciences	12	17	29	38
Technology and natural sciences	26	14	42	10
Unknown	2	0	5	15
Total	99	100	100	101
	(N=91)	(N=94)	(N=65)	(N=61)

[a] CS=US Career civil servants.
[b] PE=US political executives.

Source: J.D. Aberbach, R.D. Putnam and B.A. Rockman (1981) *Bureaucrats and Politicians in Western Democracies*, reprinted by permission of Harvard University Press, Cambridge, Mass.

including the numerically dominant lower grades) is relatively representative of the nation as a whole in terms of social and, in the United States, ethnic background, the higher the rank of the civil service one examines, the greater the over-representation of high status social and ethnic backgrounds. However, one should not dwell upon the unrepresentativeness of the civil service because the whole question of 'representative bureaucracy' is one which is riddled with theoretical and empirical problems. Expectations that the higher levels of the civil service should be representative are generally accompanied by few theoretical reasons for using the criteria of 'representativeness' that they do use. There is little convincing empirical evidence to suggest any particularly important consequences of an 'unrepresentative' civil service. The theoretical justification for a focus on representative bureaucracy is a weak one since the relationship between social background, political attitudes and behaviour is at best very circuitous. Further, the issue of the social background of senior officials is one that is not important to many theoretical approaches to bureaucracy, including those of Marx and Weber (Suleiman 1974: 158).

There is little support for the contention that higher status social background produces a senior civil service with a strongly conservative ideological bias, unless one construes the term so broadly as to include all political views that support the structures and procedures of liberal democracies. Our knowledge of the precise values held by top civil servants is admittedly sparse. Wynia (1974: 157), for example, commented that we know more about a 'typical executive's physical and historical characteristics, almost down to hair and eye color' than we do about 'such gross characteristics as political party or organizational affiliations'. Yet none of the available evidence warrants a conclusion that top civil servants share a common right-wing ideology. Aberbach, Putnam and Rockman (1981: 124) conclude from their rather limited survey data that top officials as a group are only 'slightly more conservative' than members of legislatures; while in the United States career officials 'stand slightly to the left of the average Congressman'. This conclusion is supported by other studies (Suleiman 1974; Mayntz 1978; Rose 1981).

However, the type of *educational* background of top officials is of relevance since it throws light on the type of specialist education received by officials, and consequently the degree to which officials can be expected to have influence because of their specialist knowledge. In Britain the number of senior officials without a univerisity degree is substantially higher, at 16 per cent, than any other country. Table 2.1 shows the importance of a law background for high civil service office reflecting the persistence of a *Juristenmonopol* (lawyers' monopoly) in the higher civil service in Germany, since 'Germans have for a long time believed that a legal training imparts the necessary qualifications for the higher civil service' (Mayntz 1978: 150). In Britain, on the other hand, a humanities background has long been seen as the basis for the 'generalist' administrator criticised by the Fulton Commission (1968) and its disciples (cf. Kellner and Crowther Hunt 1980).

The United States shows an equally strong bias towards the natural sciences among its top civil servants and to the social sciences among its political executives, and would appear to conform most closely to the ideal type.

If one interprets a 'specialist' training to be a training in a particular professional discipline, including the social sciences and law as well as the natural sciences, as opposed to a general arts discipline, then the country that conforms least to the Weberian ideal type is Britain. However, the argument that technical training is specialist training for the job that civil servants do is a dubious one. As Suleiman (1978) suggests, in the case of France, where the education provided in the *Grandes Écoles* is frequently assumed to be highly specialist, the training civil servants receive at the ENA has little to do with the type of work they subsequently do, nor is it particularly specialised. Similar questions about the 'specialist' training of lawyers in Germany and natural scientists in the United States could be raised.

Yet, for Weber, specialist knowledge is not simply a matter of technical training, although Weber does stress training. The knowledge that makes the ideal typical official powerful is not simply technical knowledge:

Technical knowledge alone does not guarantee the power of the official. In addition there is the knowledge of concrete facts crucial for his behaviour: knowledge of the service [*Dienstwissen*]. This is imparted to the official alone through the administrative apparatus (Weber 1972: 855).

The fact that civil servants have a career in the civil service suggests that they have been in the service a long time by the time they occupy senior positions: the officials in the Aberbach, Putnam and Rockman study (1981: 68) had been in the service on average for 28 years in Britain, 21 years in Germany, 22 years in France, and 23 years in the United States. In so far as a specialist knowledge is one based on service experience, civil servants have upwards of twenty years' apprenticeship in this field. As Rosen (1981: 204) writes: 'career executives are usually experts in a particular subject, they know the "territory", the laws, the interested power centers, and what has worked or failed and why.'

The degree to which civil servants have experience in a similar sort of job within the civil service, and are in this sense specialists, is highly variable. In Britain the service-wide character of the open structure, as well as the norms of the civil service, militate against specialisation (cf. Heclo and Wildavsky 1981), whereas in America the fact that the hiring of the official is conducted by the agency itself, characterised by Ridley (1983) as a 'job' system rather than a 'career' system, as well as the importance of acquiring a reputation in a particular policy area (see Heclo 1978), mean that 'specialization provides greater promise for advancement than does the generalist role'. This was one of the problems encountered in the setting-up in 1978 of the Senior Executive Service which was intended to create a more mobile group of senior executives (Ring and Perry 1983). Similarly, in Germany, where a *Laufbahn* (career path) is usually made within one particular field of expertise, one particular *Ressort*, and where, as in the United States, the ministry is the hiring agency, there is only a weak concept of a *service*-wide career (see Seidentopf 1980; Koenig 1983). These factors make the degree of specialisation in this sense greater in Germany than in Britain. The system of the

Grands Corps offers at the same time mobility and the pursuit of a specialised career (see Thoenig 1973, for an excellent discussion of this). On the one hand, for many members of the *corps* they will remain within one ministry, yet the principle of *détachement*, the secondment of a civil servant to a ministry not dominated by his *corps* (see Suleiman 1974: 241ff), makes mobility highly desirable for career improvement. Consequently, as Catherine Grémion (1979) suggests, the most active policy-making group of senior civil servants in France are those who are '*hors machine*'—those whose mobility has freed them from the constraints upon the ability to make decisions which *corps* loyalties and specialisation place upon the majority of civil servants.

THE ROLE OF OFFICIALS

Weber is frequently interpreted as stating that there is an ideal-type distinction between making policy and carrying it out. Diamant (1962: 84–5), for example, argues that one of the major criticisms of Weber's approach is that it claimed that 'politicians in parliament and cabinet were to make policy while bureaucrats were to carry out the orders of their political bosses and were never to be entrusted with policy-making functions' (see also Peters 1981). Of course, one of the difficulties of this separation between policy-making and carrying out policy is that there is no real definition of what 'policy' is (e.g. it may be, among other things, what government intends or what government actually does), or what 'making' it is. Pressman and Wildavsky's (1973) classic study of implementation focused academic attention upon the degree to which events in the implementation stage of the policy process shape the actual outcome of a policy decision or set of policy decisions. Those lower down in the hierarchy, including Lipsky's (1979) 'street level bureaucrats' (referring to doctors, teachers, social workers and policemen among others), can be termed 'policy-makers' according to some definitions of the term. Others (see Barrett and Fudge 1981) regard the distinction between policy and implementation as artificial, preferring to see the policy process as a 'policy-action' *continuum* shaped by a variety of actors at different levels within an organisation (or indeed within an interorganisational network).

However, there is clear evidence that what is indisputably part of policy-making, by almost any definition, such as making public expenditure decisions, is something that senior officials do, or at least play an important part in. Evidence of this is spread throughout a number of studies such as the US Advisory Commission on Intergovernmental Relations (1981a, b) study on the growth of government in the United States which offered some support for the hypothesis that officials helped shape the nature of welfare programmes over the past twenty-five years. Similar examples of civil servants influencing policy-making can be found in Hockert's (1980) study of social policy in the immediate post-war period in Germany, Richardson and Jordan's (1979) textbook on Britain and Hayward's (1983) textbook on France. To seek to compile a list of cases in which civil servants have made policy would be arduous work and make tedious reading. Furthermore, the fact that between 80 and 90 per cent of civil servants see their role as 'policy-makers' in the three European nations (Aberbach, Putnam and Rockman 1981: 97) suggests that civil servants are prepared to admit that they make policy. Although the precise numbers are not presented in Aberbach, Putnam and Rockman's (1981) study, from elsewhere in the study (e.g. pp. 96–100) and from other studies (Heclo 1977: 148–53) there is no reason to suggest that American career officials or political executives should be less likely to regard themselves as policy-makers than their European counterparts. The widespread acceptance of the policy-making role of civil servants is well illustrated by the reaction of two British journalists to a British civil servant's claim that 'power stems from the people and flows through Parliament to the minister responsible to Parliament'; Young and Sloman (1981: 20) felt compelled to add: 'listening to that you'd have no reason to know that [this man], a Permanent Secretary before he was fifty, is reputed to be one of the most brilliant men in Whitehall.'

This would appear to provide overwhelming evidence to support Diamant's criticism of Weber—none of the civil services in our four countries has career officials whose roles conform to the 'politicans decide, officials carry out' model ascribed to Weber. However, such an interpretation misses the thrust of Weber's differentiation between politics and administration. Weber's distinction between officials and politicians was not identical to the rather unsatisfactory distinction between policy-making and its execution frequently (and more accurately) associated with Woodrow Wilson. Weber (1958: 322–3) recognised that officials may adopt policy-making roles when he wrote:

The difference [between politicians and officials] lies only in part in what is expected of each of them. Independence of judgement and the ability to impose one's own ideas are very often expected of officials as well as political leaders. Even the notion that the official spends his time dealing with subordinate matters of routine and leaders do the interesting intellectual jobs is a conceit, and could only be imagined in a country which has no insight into how its public affairs are conducted and its officials work. No, the answer lies in the type of responsibility of each, and it is this which to all intents and purposes shapes the demands placed on each.

The official has ideas and imagination (*Vorstellungen*), yet he must, if his superiors insist, accept the orders of hierarchical superiors as overriding his own, and 'do his duty as if he were carrying out his own most personal convictions' (Weber 1958: 323). A political leader

who acted in this way would earn nothing but scorn. He often has to make compromises, i.e. sacrifice the less for the more important. If he does not have the courage to say either this goes through or I resign, then he is a wretched 'clinger' (*Kleber*), as Bismarck named this sort of person, and not a leader. . . The struggle for personal power and the resulting *personal responsibility for one's own sphere* is the essence of the politician as well as the capitalist entrepreneur.

When viewed from this perspective there is some evidence that the three European countries in this comparison do conform to the Weberian ideal type. The Aberbach, Putnam and Rockman (1981: 97) study shows that few civil servants (4 per cent in Britain, 1 per cent in France, 12 per cent in Germany) perceived their role as 'partisans'. They conclude:

Politicians especially orient themselves toward partisan politics, toward representing groups, and toward advocating causes, role foci that are largely foreign to bureaucrats. Bureaucrats are far more apt to focus instead on applying technical expertise to the solution of problems, a role with little resonance among politicians. From these data the Weberian distinction between the world of the bureaucrat and that of the politician is well sustained. (Aberbach, Putnam and Rockman 1981: 89)

In the United States, however there is a greater emphasis upon a partisan role among civil servants, with 24 per cent of the sample of civil servants seeing their role as partisan, while only 13 per cent of Congressmen saw their role in these terms.

CONCLUSION

The recruitment patterns of senior officials differ in each of the four countries examined in this study. Only in Britain and France can senior officials be relatively accurately described as career officials. In the United States senior posts are manned by political appointees who may have had little experience in government organisations. This argument should not be pushed too far since political executives are not invariably newcomers to national government (Heclo 1977: 100), and they may have acquired expertise in a particular policy field as members of 'issue networks'. Yet, as Heclo (1970: 100–1) comments, compared with civil servants, the government experience of 'the men and women coming to top political positions naturally seems meager'. In Germany, senior posts are in principle subject to ministerial appointment, although there are constraints which result in these appointments being conferred largely on civil servants. Furthermore, the degree to which one can call the promotion of officials 'merit' varies, with non-merit criteria (if the favour of a minister can be so termed) being found in each of the four countries to varying degrees. Training is not unambiguously 'specialist' in any of the four countries, the popular perceptions of the French system of civil service training notwithstanding.

How far, then, does the job of the official correspond to the Weberian ideal type? The answer must be that it does so sufficiently closely to justify asking the same questions about the scope for political leadership in a bureaucratic system as Weber did. In the three European countries career officials are permanent, and while their technical training is highly variable, the fact that they are experienced officials means that they almost inevitably have *Dienstwissen* (knowledge of the service), even if it is accepted that technical training in terms of a science or law degree does not constitute a professional vocational training for the top official. Even in the case of political appointees in the European countries, one finds constraints upon those making appointments which lead them to choose permanent officials for political appointee posts. This has led some to comment that political appointments are just as likely to constitute a 'bureaucratisation of politics' rather than a 'politicisation' of bureaucracy (cf. Dyson 1977; Birnbaum 1982).

In the United States, top political executives are not routinely recruited from within the career service. Yet this does not detract from posing the question about the relationship between appointees and their officials whose influence is based upon the expertise that they have gained from familiarity with their jobs and the Washington scene. The same question that Weber posed of the scope for political leadership in a system in which the political leader is dependent upon skilled and knowledgeable officials is posed, albeit at a different level within the hierarchy of the government structure in the United States. Heclo's (1977: 235) study shows this very clearly; not only do political executives in America have to learn how to 'help themselves but also how to acquire help from powerful and valuable subordinates in their own organization', whose power derives to a large extent from their familiarity with the institution in which they work and its environment.

3   Competences and Hierarchy

Weber's analysis stresses the importance of a clear division
of competences as well as a 'firmly ordered system of
superiority and subordination among authorities with the
supervision of the former by the latter' (Weber 1972: 551) as
a factor distinguishing the modern rational-legal bureaucratic system of rule from traditional forms of rule in which such
features may indeed have been present, but were exceptions
to the general pattern. Here, the term 'competences' is used
in a legal context found frequently in German law. It refers
to the possession of legally-defined powers and obligations.
This stress upon the division of competences and hierarchy
ties in closely with Weber's use of the term 'rationality'. As
Mayntz (1965) points out, the term 'rationality' has been
interpreted by organisational sociologists to refer to notions
of 'efficiency' in organisations and formed the basis of an
organisational sociology critique of Weber.
  It is not difficult to see how a strict definition of
competences within a hierarchically ordered administrative
staff could lead to 'inefficiency'; for example, the continual
referral of minute decisions to a central administrative
authority causes delay and unnecessary work, as for example
it did in the case of a local authority which took two years to
secure permission from central government for the provision
of a hutted day nursery (Institute of Public Administration
1948). Thus, Weber's insistence upon hierarchy and clear
delineation of competences has been argued to lead to
'inefficiency'. Blau and Meyer (1971: 26) for example,
suggest that,

Since the ideal type is conceived as the perfectly efficient organisation, all differences from it must necessarily interfere with that efficiency. There is considerable evidence that suggests an opposite conclusion; informal relations and unofficial practices often contribute towards efficient operations.

However, to evaluate Weber's theory in such a context is misleading. Weber's conception of rationality was concerned with specification of means for defined ends, and here the defined end was 'the continual and technically efficient exercise of legal authority—as a further qualification one might add that this refers to conditions prevailing in an economically developed and politically centralised nation state' (Mayntz 1965).

It is not important that bureaucratic organisations contain clear delineation of competences and a clear hierarchical relationship simply in order that one can distinguish bureaucratic from traditional systems of government. If political leaders are expected to use the administrative apparatus as a machine which 'normally carries on functioning for a revolutionary movement which comes to power by force, or an enemy's army of occupation, in just the same way as it did for the previous legal government' (Weber 1972: 128), then it must be capable of being operated as a machine with, to pursue the analogy, clearly identifiable levers which work in a predictable way when pulled. In order for a political leader to give direction to the administrative staff, the existence of a hierarchy establishes both the legitimacy of the leadership and guarantees that a leader's decision will be reflected in the behaviour of the members of the administration. The clear definition of competences allows the political leadership to identify what a particular organisation can do.

One way in which the development of a hierarchically structured monocratic system of bureaucratic government can increase the power of the official is that when officials gain power within it they are at the apex of a powerful organisation which can be commanded by a relatively small group of officials. However, the opposite does not necessarily follow. If bureaucratic organisation falls far short of the monocratic principle rule by officials may still be found, but

it will be of a different type from that found in a monocratic
system.

Given the fact that the modern bureaucratic organisation
is based upon the division of labour, and that officials in
bureaucracies are expected to display initiative in their
everyday work (see Chapter 2), there is a tendency within
bureaucracies to develop into fragmented groups of organisations which operate independently of each other and
have the potential for conflict with each other. Weber's
discussion of the experience of the bureaucracies of Imperial
Germany and Imperial Russia indicates a belief that modern
bureaucracies contain a tendency towards 'satrapic' (referring to the territorial potentates of Ancient Persia) conflicts
between different parts of the state administration. In
Imperial Russia as well as Imperial Germany conflicts
between different branches (*Ressorts*) of the administration
were one of the main reasons for the absence of control over
them (Weber 1972: 573). In the absence of genuine political
leadership, far from weakening the position of the administrative staff, conflicts between different sectors of the
administration may limit the degree to which the administrative staff can be controlled.

At issue in these satrapic conflicts between the different parts of
the administrative staff are not only technical (*sachlich*) factors,
but also personal differences. . . . It is not technical considerations
or political leadership qualities which then decide who gains the
upper hand, but courtly intrigues. (Weber 1958: 326)

Weber does not, however, regard the tendency for policy
outcomes to reflect satrapic conflicts as inevitable within
modern bureaucracies. The tendency to divide into a variety
of powerful, and sometimes conflictual, groups emerges in
the absence of political leadership within a governmental
system (i.e. where the particular type of ministerial leader
described by Weber is not found; see Chapters 2 and 7), and
the absence of any effective form of collegial authority over
the administrative staff. To explore the degree of differentiation within a bureaucratic system on its own is not to
suggest that it has an uncontrollable administration, thus

equating any internal differentiation within them to the satrapic conflicts discussed by Weber in the context of Germany and Russia.

However, in order to assess the nature and limitations of political leadership (see Chapter 7), it is important to examine the degree to which administrative organisations in each of the countries conform to the ideal-typical model of clear competences and hierarchy, since these help define the nature of the challenges to political leadership within them. The development of differentiated organisations in which competences are not clearly defined, and in which behaviour does not conform to a simple top-down monocratic model of hierarchy, poses problems for political leadership of a different sort from those posed by a cohesive official elite commanding a monolithic bureaucratic organisation. Fragmentation and the monocratic principle pose different threats to the exercise of political leadership, and it is the ability of political leadership to exert authority within either a monocratically structured or an internally differentiated system which determines the degree to which either results in rule by officials.

THE DIVISION OF COMPETENCES

Under no circumstances could any of the administrative systems of each of the four polities examined in this study be classified as simple in structure. Perhaps the most striking form of organisational diversity and complexity is found in the case of the United States, where there is not only a large number of distinct federal organisations, but also a great variety of types of organisations and types of criteria that could be used to distinguish one organisation from another such that the precise number of federal government organisations is contentious. Seidman's (1980: 236–40) 'not necessarily complete list' includes 14 executive departments, 10 offices within the Executive Office of the President, 25 independent agencies, 2 foundations, 17 institutions and institutes, 2 claims commissions, 13 regulatory commissions, 45 government corporations, 6 inter-agency boards, 4 statutory advisory bodies, 4 joint executive–congressional commissions, 13 intergovernmental (i.e. joint federal–state) organisations, 13 organisations in the 'twilight zone' and 14 institutions 'organised and financed by the federal government to provide contractual services'. Kaufman (1981a: 5–6) argues that there is no generally accepted way of knowing how many distinctive government organisations, 'bureaus', there are in the American federal government because of the diverse organisational principles applied throughout the federal administration.

The systems of administration in the West European countries are no less complex, despite the apparent simplicity of the division into a small number of ministries and departments. In Britain, Hood and Dunsire (1981: 40) found, like Kaufman, that 'there appears to be no single stipulative definition of what constitutes a "department", in official use in Whitehall'. The system is complex because there are a variety of different non-departmental organisations, so-called 'quangos' (see Barker 1982), and because within government departments it is possible to distinguish between different organisational sub-units which are nominally part of the same ministry. One obvious example of this would be the distinctiveness of the health and the social security sides of the Department of Health and Social Security (see Garrett 1980: 73). One could even go further and divide government organisations into a plethora of groups fulfilling different tasks, and regard these as distinctive organisations (Pitt and Smith 1981: 60–85). As Hood and Dunsire point out (1981: 41), the scope for distinguishing within British ministries a large number of discrete organisations is large since the official year book of the civil service for 1975 gave 'a total of no less than 787 bodies in its "Index of Departments and Sub-Departments"'.

Similar observations of complexity can be found in Germany and France. There is a variety of distinctive types of organisations which do not conform to the model of all central government civil servants being organised within a ministerial structure, as with the *établissements publics* in France (including, for example, the *Centre National de la Recherche Scientifique* which organises and funds higher research in France) or the *Anstalten des öffentlichen Rechts* in Germany (e.g. the *Bundesanstalt für Arbeit*, the federal employment office). As in Britain and the United States, the ministries themselves in France and Germany could be divided into distinctive organisations or bureaus. Darbel and Schnapper (1969: 72) note the absence of a common terminology to describe the different sub-units of French ministries, and show how ministries are composed of a variety of distinct *directions* and *sous-directions*; while Scharpf, Reissert and Schnabel (1976: 18–20) point to the institutional fragmentation that arises from specialisation within the German federal bureaucracy.

Few would expect the organisation of government to be otherwise than complex since, as Weber points out, modern bureaucratic organisation is based upon the modern organi-sational principle of the division of labour. Furthermore, this complexity coexists with an *interdependence* between different organisations within government, by which is meant that one particular organisation, whether it be a ministry or a sub-division of a ministry, cannot fulfil its tasks without the collaboration of another. Classic examples of this would include the fifteen separate ministries responsible for development aid in Germany in the 1960s (Rausch 1976: 191), the interdependence between medium- and long-term planning agencies and short-term budget agencies in France (Green 1981), or the complex dispersion of regional industrial development incentives across a range of government departments and other public bodies (Hogwood 1982). Kaufman's (1981a: 62) detailed examination of the working life of federal bureau chiefs gives striking evidence of the interdependence between separate government orga-nisations:

The number of points of tangency of the bureaus was striking. [The Customs Service] for instance, counted some forty sister agencies helped by customs officers to guard against illegal entry of forbidden and controlled substances and even against illegal immigration. . . . Similarly, the Animal and Plant Health Inspec-tion Service worked with the Food and Drug Administration on keeping carcinogens from entering the food chain through additives to animal feed . . . and with the State Department on fashioning agreements with foreign governments to prevent the importation of . . . pests and diseases from abroad and to permit the exportation of American foodstuffs.

Furthermore, as Wildavsky (1979) suggests, there are sound theoretical reasons to expect the interdependence and overlap between different government organisations to increase with the expansion of governmental functions. As the policy space becomes increasingly filled—that is to say, the more and more areas of social and economic life that are subject to governmental programmes or regulation—the more likely that the effects of one governmental action will impinge upon another and through the search for remedial measures policy becomes its 'own cause' (see also Beer 1978; Heclo 1978).

One must avoid presenting a picture of permanent conflicts between interdependent government organisations, since conflict-avoiding strategies are probably far more common a means of resolving policy differences (see Scharpf, Reissert and Schnabel 1976) than open conflict. Yet conflicts do emerge between government organisations. There are certainly plenty of examples of conflicts and uncertainties over spheres of competence of different organisations. The division of competences, for example, between long-term planning agencies and short-term finance ministries, has produced conflicts over the valid role of each. In France, Green (1981: 104) discusses the 'permanent battle' which the finance ministry has waged 'to contain the inflation which inevitably resulted from the growth-oriented policies pursued by the [Planning] Commission'. In Britain, Heclo and Wildavsky (1981: 210) point to the conflicts between the Treasury and the short-lived Department of Economic Affairs over the respective role of each in the management of the economy. More recently in Britain, the rivalry between the Department of Health and Social Security and the Department of the Environment over the administration of housing benefits contributed to the creation of a housing benefit system widely regarded as inefficient and the cause of substantial hardship to those entitled to benefits (*The Times*, 20 January 1984). Thoenig and Friedberg's (1976) study showed how reforms in the 1960s aimed at merging ministries in order to produce a more integrated organisational machinery to deal with urban planning in France were influenced by officials in the public works ministry who sought to use the reforms to enhance their own status and prestige at the expense of the housing ministry. As a consequence 'the merger of local agencies seemed rather like a take-over of Housing by Public Works' (Thoenig and Friedberg 1976: 328). In Germany, Hockerts (1980: 118–19) warns of placing too much credence upon the judgement of commentators who suggested that post-war social welfare policy was bedevilled by demarcation disputes or 'turf' conflicts between a variety of different ministries, but does suggest that the overlap of competences between the family ministry and the labour ministry 'strengthened the ability of interest groups to manoeuvre'. In the United States, Seidman (1980: 204) points out that conflicts such as that between the National Park Service and the Army Corps of Engineers over Florida's Everglades National Park are widely interpreted as indicating a need for greater 'coordination' among federal agencies.

How far do these interdependencies, which involve the possibility of conflict, reflect overlaps of competences rather than the outcome of a simple division of labour? Unfortunately, it is impossible to test precisely how far there is a clear division of competences in the bureaucratic systems of each of the four countries individually, let alone comparatively. Such an exercise would require, ideally speaking, a comprehensive list of competences of each government organisation in each country from which could be computed the number of duplications. Since we have no definition of government organisations, and since defining the functions of organisations is even more problematic (see Hogwood and Peters 1982), we are unlikely ever to have a satisfactory assessment of the degree of clarity in the allocation of government functions. The discussion of the division of competences in Weber is probably more useful in distinguishing modern bureaucratic systems from their traditional predecessors rather than in distinguishing between different modern systems. Nevertheless, it is important to point out that allocation of competences is only clear relative to the impenetrable complexity of traditional systems of government. In modern bureaucratic systems competences are frequently unclear and disputed between government organisations. This suggests that, if there is rule by officials, to characterise it as a single top-level élite controlling a cohesive bureaucratic machine is inappropriate. A more real threat to political leadership is the problem of giving direction to a variety of differentiated organisations within the bureaucratic system.

HIERARCHY AND TOP-DOWN POLICY-MAKING

The notion of 'top-down' policy-making implies that the importance of a decision is perfectly correlated to the hierarchical level at which it is taken. Thus we would expect the most important policy decisions to be taken at the apex of a government organisation, whether by a politician or official, and those lower down in the hierarchy merely to carry them out. There is overwhelming evidence to suggest that this is not the way in which government works. Important decisions are taken at different levels within the hierarchy of government organisations.

Kaufman's (1981a: 19–20) study of US federal bureau chiefs offers perhaps the most systematic evidence of the frequency with which important policy decisions are taken by relatively junior personnel, frequently without being reviewed by hierarchical superiors:

The Hollywood image of executives firing off critical decisions in machine-gun fashion is far removed from the reality of executive life as I saw it. . . . In all the bureaus, numerous decisions emerged from the interactions of subordinates at all levels, in the field as well as in headquarters, that would have to be regarded as important by even a stringent definition of significance. . . . Yet only a small fraction of them were issued or even reviewed by the chiefs themselves.

While we lack similar analytical studies of the everyday

life of heads of a selection of administrative agencies in the other three countries, there is nevertheless evidence to suggest that the conscious or unknowing delegation of important policy decisions to those lower down in the hierarchy of organisations is fairly commonplace. In Heclo and Wildavsky's study of the Treasury (1981: 118–28) it is the Principal Finance Officer, usually an Under-Secretary or less frequently a Deputy Secretary in a government department, who routinely deals with the Treasury and negotiates for the department's allocation of funds from the Treasury. Similarly in France, Catherine Grémion (1982: 215) points out that the reform of housing finance in the 1970s was a reform based on the initiative of a 'small group of men at a strictly administrative level—relatively low grade officials'; and in Germany Mayntz and Scharpf (1975: 83) show that initiatives frequently originate at subordinate levels within the German administrative structure.

This argument, that important decisions do not solely emanate from the senior positions within the formal hierarchy of government organisations, could be extended to include a whole range of lower-grade officials, the field staff or 'front line administrators', as participants in policy-making. The implications of the actions of lower level officials for national policies became prominent in the academic field of public policy studies following Pressman and Wildavsky's (1973) study of the Economic Development Administration project in Oakland. This study, as its sub-title ('How Great Expectations in Washington are dashed in Oakland') suggests, showed how those involved in carrying out policies have a crucial role to play in the shaping of the policy as well, as in its success or failure. Since then there has been a great variety of studies (see Wolman 1981) which show how implementation problems affect policy outcomes. Only rarely do such problems result from conscious obstruction, more frequently they result from the pursuit of self-interest on the part of those in the field implementing programmes. The relative isolation from direct supervision of a number of 'front line' officials, (teachers, policemen, doctors) was at the heart of Lipsky's *Street Level Bureaucracy* (1979) thesis. Lipsky argued that the nature of the work of the street level bureaucrats, acting on their own initiative in surroundings remote from centres of hierarchical authority, gave them a high degree of autonomy from hierarchical control.

However, hierarchy does not imply the ability to trace all policy decisions of any import unambiguously to the top of the organisational pyramid, and Weber's (1958: 322–3) acknowledgement of the importance of subordinate officials underlines this. Rather, the existence of hierarchy must be interpreted as the *ability* of a superior organisation or an official in a superior position to review the actions of a subordinate and give the subordinate directions. Each of the administrative systems of the four countries can be described as hierarchical in this limited sense. There are different ranks of personnel, and superiors have the authority to give directions to their subordinates. There are obviously exceptions to this, as in the case of the US Cabinet Secretaries whose hierarchical powers over their component bureaus and agencies appear limited, above all by congressional expectations that the Cabinet Secretary will not intervene in their affairs. For example, one Secretary of Agriculture 'had his knuckles rapped' by Congress for invoking his statutory authority to approve the loans of the Rural Electrification Administration (Seidman 1980: 163–4).

The importance of hierarchy within government organisations is unlikely to emerge in a particularly visible form; rather, it is more likely to take the form of subordinates anticipating the reactions of hierarchical superiors. This is similar to what Sharpe (1976) termed the 'operating ideology' in the somewhat different context of relationships between councillors and officers in British local government. It is mistaken to look for direct assertion of authority in order to establish its existence. To do so is to forget that the subordinate is likely to have some idea of the predispositions and values of his superior, and know the constraints within which his superior operates. A subordinate is unlikely to waste time making proposals which will then be flatly rejected. Mayntz and Scharpf (1975: 101) describe the more common pattern of interaction between superior and subordinate:

The chances of success of the proposal [of a lower grade official] are low where top-level support is needed, but cannot be gained, for a project, and swimming against the stream of executive opinion may be costly in terms of one's own career. Realizing this, and generally not being much inclined to escape executive control, the subordinate ranks attempt to anticipate executive reactions to the projects they seem to develop without intervention and guidance from the top.

Similar processes of anticipating reactions have been identified in France (Suleiman 1974), Britain (Heclo and Wildavsky 1981) and the United States (Heclo 1977).

While hierarchy, in the sense of being able to claim authority to review the actions of subordinates, is pervasive, it should not be assumed that invoking hierarchical superiority is a particularly common means of conducting relationships within the executive. This is not only because the effect of hierarchy is avoided through the anticipation of reactions, but also because under certain circumstances the effectiveness of hierarchical superiority as a means of securing influence can be limited. This appears to be especially clearly the case in the United States. To use hierarchical rank consistently as a means of getting one's own way suggests that the superior is unwilling to listen to the advice of his subordinates. One official in Heclo's study (1977: 172) explains how the practice of 'pulling rank' can be used against the hierarchical superior:

If [a certain political executive] wants to order hemlock, they'll let him have it. If he wants a new air conditioner they'll do it and not tell him it will cause the ceiling to collapse; he'll just come in one day and see the building half torn down and when people start complaining, there will be his order—in writing

To secure influence in face-to-face relationships requires more than simple recourse to hierarchical rank. In the United States the limitations on hierarchical authority and the need to build up trust and confidence are especially apparent in the case of the political appointees who formally head government departments and agencies. Heclo contrasts the 'ideal world' of clearly-defined and accepted hierarchical relationships and competences with the realities of working conditions in Washington which 'few would mistake for an ideal realm' (Heclo 1977: 154).

Similar observations can be made about the three European nations. For example, in Britain, in the case of conflicts between the British government departments, hierarchical rank can be used as one means of asserting influence, as Heclo and Wildavsky (1981: 125) show. Yet it is not one that can be persistently used on its own. The continual overruling by the Permanent Secretary of the Principal Finance Officer may produce a counter-reaction: 'the finance officer may help people in the Treasury challenge the Permanent Secretary's views.' As Heclo and Wildavsky point out, the whole ethos of the 'private government of public money' in Whitehall is one based upon a high degree of trust. In Germany, Dyson (1977) showed that unpopular political appointees were unable to establish authority within their own departments; and Mayntz and Scharpf's (1975) discussion of the albeit imperfectly developed 'dialogue' among top executives, career and political, was characterised by the bargaining and the anticipation of reactions of different actors in the policy process. In France, Suleiman's (1974) study shows the need for the *directeur* to build up trust with the minister's *cabinet* in order to exercise influence.

While executive departments and agencies constitute a complex and segmented set of organisations, their *internal* structure can be termed hierarchical in the sense that a superior is able to review decisions and actions of a subordinate. The fact that government rarely works in this way (that is to say, through the routine application of hierarchical authority) does not detract from its existence. Neither does the fact that the relationship with groups outside the executive, notably the legislature (see Chapter 4) and interest groups (Chapter 5), constrains the degree to which senior members of government agencies, whether career or non-career, can apply their hierarchical authority. As van Riper (1983: 488) writes, even in the United States 'the executive is as well equipped administratively now as the instrument panel of a 747 plane. The problem lies with the co-pilots, the Congress and the party system.' The

executive organisations of government do not constitute a
single hierarchy in any of the four countries in this study,
and there are constraints on the use of hierarchical authority. Yet the hierarchical principle of government organisation is sufficiently pervasive that those who occupy the
senior posts within the organisation can expect to affect
significantly policy-making within it.

TERRITORIAL DIFFERENTIATION, FUNCTIONS AND HIERARCHY

The division of functions and the hierarchy discussed so far
have referred only to one portion of the administrative staff
of government: the central civil service. A further dimension
to the degree to which the administrative apparatus represents a machine is found in the territorial division of
responsibilities. Although Weber (1958: 394–431) discussed
extensively the role of the specific federal arrangements and
above all the dominance of Prussia in the Imperial German
system, one would be hard pressed to find a coherent theory
of federalism or territorial decentralisation in his writing.
However, the importance of federalism and decentralisation
for this discussion lies in the fact that a significant portion of
officials are employed outside central ministries or bodies
over which central or federal bodies exert a more or less
powerful influence. The territorial division of competences
and the hierarchical relations between national government
and territorial government pose similar questions about the
degree to which direction can be given to the governmental
administrative apparatus to those posed in the context of the
hierarchical structure of central government organisation.

The territorial arrangements through which services are
delivered outside the organisation of central government are
highly varied, as are the institutions responsible for their
delivery. Social security in France is administered through a
system of local *Caisses de Securité Sociale*, health in
Germany through the local *Ortskrankenkassen*, and in
Britain through a system of local health authorities. In the
United States some states have separate territorial boards

for water provision, while in others this is a function of some form of local government. This section is devoted to an examination of the degree to which state and local government in the United States and West Germany and local government in France and Britain are hierarchically integrated into their respective bureaucratic systems.

While state and local governments are not the only form of non-central government employers, they are one of the most important (see Table 3.1). In 1980 local government employed 23 per cent of public employees in France, 38 per cent in Britain, and state and local government 41 per cent in Germany, and 70 per cent in the United States. Only in France, where teachers are central government employees, does the central government employ more than local government; in the other three countries around three times as many government employees are employed by state and local government as are employed by the central or federal government.

Table 3.1 Central, state and local employees 1980 (%)

	US	Germany	France	Britain
Central/federal	22	13	45	14
State and/or local	70	41	23	38
Other[a]	8	56	32	48
	100	100	100	100

[a] Includes employees in public enterprises and non-municipal health services.

Source: Rose (forthcoming). Printed by kind permission of the author.

The structure of state and local government in each of the four countries is relatively simply described. The fifty states in the United States have a constitutional claim to sovereignty within the federal constitution. Local government organisation is a responsibility of the states and different states have different constitutions as regards the organisation of local government. However, in the United States as a whole there was, in 1977, a total of 79,863 local authorities including 3042 counties, 18,863 municipalities, 16,822 townships, 15,174 school districts and 25,962 special districts. Similarly in West Germany, the eight states have responsibility for the structure and organisation of local government and the two city states of Hamburg and Bremen have both state and local responsibilities. There are, in the whole of the Federal Republic, 235 *Kreise* (counties), 91 *Kreisfreie Städte* (county boroughs), and around 8200 *Gemeinde* (individual small area local authority districts) (Albertin 1983: 92). The two *Stadstaaten*, the city states of Hamburg and Bremen, have no form of local government equivalent to that found elsewhere in Germany. In France, as implied in the term 'unitary state', local government structure and organisation is formally a responsibility of central government. The local government system of France consists of over 36,000 *communes* and the various partnerships formed of these *communes*, such as the *communautés urbaines* in the cities, aimed primarily to devise policies for the *communes* of a wider metropolitan area, or the *syndicats des communes* which are often no more than arrangements made by two or more individual *communes* jointly to provide certain specific services. In Britain the local government system consists of the 522 counties, districts, London boroughs, the City of London, the Greater London Council, the Scottish regions, districts and islands.

What state and local governments do is defined formally in both functional (that is, through definition of the services for which they are responsible) and hierarchical (that is, the degree to which they are subject to central direction) terms. This is shown clearly in the case of Britain, where broad functional responsibilities can be relatively easily outlined. Major local government functions in Britain (in Northern Ireland the 26 local government districts have few resposibilities; see Birrell and Murie 1980) include education, housing, personal social services, fire, police, transport, roads, museums and recreational facilities. There are, of course, some exceptions to this (cf. Page 1980; Elliott 1981). One major exception is central government's responsibility for police in London; and there is a host of minor exceptions—Hull, for example, has its own municipal telephone company. Scottish local government shows some differences in the range of tasks it undertakes—in contrast to elsewhere in Britain, water and sewerage is a local function, and the Scottish Education Department of the Scottish Office, the central government ministry responsible for many general government functions in Scotland (cf. Rose 1982), administers student grants for higher education. Of course, the distribution of the services between different types of local government unit is variable. For most of England and Wales the larger area county services are education, fire, police, personal social services and roads, while the districts have housing, public health and refuse collection. In metropolitan areas the districts rather than the counties have education and social service functions, and in London education is a function of the Inner London Education Authority. Most local government functions in London are exercised by the London boroughs, with the Greater London Council (GLC) having identical functions in some areas (housing and parks) as well as an overall planning function. (In 1983 the Conservative government proposed abolishing the GLC and the metropolitan counties.) In Scotland, the regional councils largely fulfil similar functions to the English counties outside the metropolitan areas.

In addition to the broad allocation of functional responsibilities, the formal hierarchical position of local authorities in Britain is that they are constitutional inferiors to central government. Local government only provides the services it does because it has been given powers to do so, and the doctrine of *ultra vires* prevents it from actions not formally approved by law. In addition, central government has powers to *mandate*— to require by law that a local authority do something, such as sell council houses—and it can inspect local services and audit accounts. It can also reorganise the entire structure of local government.

In France, the division of competences similarly involves, at least in formal terms, the division of functions as well as a division of hierarchical competences. The precise functional responsibilities of French local governments vary, primarily according to their size. With over 36,000 *communes* it is to be expected that there are inequalities in population size, and there are many *communes* with fewer than a hundred inhabitants, and some with none. At the other extreme, Marseilles has 914,000 people and Paris 2.3 million. Local government in the smaller rural *communes* has few real services—the mayor might be able to call on the services of a few part-time firemen (*sapeurs pompiers*), but not much beyond that. In the larger *communes* a wide range of services are provided—urban transport and roads, *assistance sociale*, which includes some cash transfers as well as personal social services, school building, urban planning, public health and recreational services. In many cases the *commune*, especially the larger urban *commune*, delivers services in close collaboration with the *département* headed by the *préfet*, and/or with different forms of grouping of communes such as the *communautés urbaines*. The basic principle of functional allocation is that the localities are permitted to deliver a service unless the central state deems it to be national. On top of this broad pattern of functional allocations, the local authorities were, until the territorial reforms of the 1981 Mitterrand presidency, formally under the tutelage (*tutelle*) of central government, above all in the guise of the *préfets*, employees of the Ministry of the Interior. The decentralisation reforms of the Mitterrand government have yet to be completed, and it would be hazardous at present to offer a picture of what the legal framework of central–local relations will look like once they have been completed (see Mény 1983).

The United States comparison shows the relative simplicity of the British and French system of functional allocation of competences. Collectively, state and local governments are responsible for delivering (or at least have a major role in delivering) most government services. The postal service and defence are the only major services run exclusively by the federal government. For the other services, such as police, fire services, education, roads and transport, parks and some public utilities, the state and local governments have formal responsibility. Even in the sphere of cash support for social security, schemes are administered by state and local government, with support and direction through federal money and regulations. How these functions are divided as between state and local government is highly variable. Local government in Vermont, for example, has a relatively limited set of functions, being responsible for only 40 per cent of state and local expenditure as compared with California where local government is responsible for 75 per cent. Just as the functional division between state and local government varies, so too do the names and status of the local government units themselves. The United States system of local government system has been characterised as an 'embarrassment of riches' (Marlan 1967). The titles of books on American urban politics and government, such as Wood's (1961) study of New York, *1400 Governments*, and Fogelson's (1967) study of Los Angeles, *Fragmented Metropolis*, underline the fact that American urban government is characterised by a plethora of government units of different status covering a single metropolitan area. The use of common terms, such as 'county', 'township', 'municipality' to enumerate the number of local government units even suggests a picture of greater simplicity than exists in reality. Some sorts of local government unit are found in some states and not in others; for example, Iowa and Arizona have no townships at all. Even where local government units are nominally the same, they are very different in the types of functions they fulfil. For example, the mid-western township is very different from the New England township. Some municipalities, such as New York City, have responsibility for schools, while in most other localities more or less independent school boards, accounting for 88 per cent of school enrolments in the United States, have this responsibility.

The *formal* constitutional hierarchical division of competences can also be relatively simply described. First, the relationship between the federal and state governments is one of 'separate authority' or a 'layer cake' model of authority (Wright, D.S. 1978). This refers to the constitutional principle that the federal government (excluding the judiciary) has no direct authority to mandate or otherwise intervene in state functions. The relationship between state and local government is, according to Dillon's rule (a doctrine derived from an Iowa court decision in 1868; see Wright D.S. 1978: 20–1), analogous to the formal relationship between central and local government in unitary systems; the local government is the creature of the state and the state government has direct hierarchical superiority over it.

In Germany the formal division of responsibilities between different levels of government does not conform to the American federal model of a division of functional authority. Instead, the division of functions and the division of hierarchical competences are mixed. The predominant feature in the formal division of competences is its horizontal or hierarchical nature, referring to the ability of the federal government to assume competence for a large number of policy issues by setting broad guidelines which constrain the way in which states deliver these policies. There are broadly five types of policy areas. First those which cover exclusively federal (*Bundeseigene*) functions, such as foreign affairs and defence. Second, those functions for which states have responsibility, such as roads and environmental protection, but which are classed as areas in which the federal and state level have concurrent powers of legislation, meaning that the states have power to legislate when the federal government does not use its power to legislate. Third, there are areas traditionally within the sphere of *Land* competence but nevertheless subject to general guideline legislation (*Rahmengesetze*); for example, the legal status of *Land* officials, the framework of tertiary education and land use.

This horizontal division of competences does not apply to all policy areas. The fourth type of policy area is comprised of those functions which are almost exclusively the responsibility of state governments. In the field of police, education and local government structure vertical or functional divisions of competences apply—in these areas the supremacy of the states is acknowledged, and the federal government has at most a limited role. The German constitution was amended in 1969 to create a fifth type of policy area: 'joint tasks' (*Gemeinschaftsaufgaben*), which allowed federal government involvement (primarily through grants in aid) in areas where there was doubt over the constitutionality of federal involvement; e.g. university construction, regional and agricultural policy and coastal preservation. This has commonly been interpreted as an expansion of the role of the federation over the *Länder*. (For a critical discussion of the view see Scharpf, Reissert and Schnabel 1976).

The position of local government is, as in the United States, the responsibility of the *Länder*. Broadly, the local government units are presumed to be omnicompetent—they are allowed to provide any service unless explicitly forbidden by the *Land*. However, in the division of competences between the state and local level, a similar pattern of hierarchical differentiation can be found to that found at the federal level. While state constitutions set out what services local governments may provide—mainly consisting of primary education, public health, social services as well as municipal recreation and trading enterprises—they also state the services they must provide, although this varies from *Land* to *Land*.

Of course, the formally stated principle of the hierarchical superiority of central and, for some policy areas, federal government in the West European systems and the formally stated principle of state autonomy from the federal level in the United States offers misleading pictures of the actual relationships between different levels of government. In France, the formal relationship of *tutelle* as a description of the actual relationship between central and local government, with its implication of the *préfet* acting as the *empereur au petit pied* and commanding local authorities, received its first major criticism with Worms' (1966) path-breaking study. Worms argued that the relationship between the *préfet* and the local *notables* (prominent figures in the locality), especially the local mayors, was one of mutual dependence. In order for the *préfet* to be successful in his own job, in order for him to have a positive role in encouraging local authorities to undertake projects, and in order to allow him to run his *département sans histoires* (i.e. without any overt political conflict), he needed the support of the mayor. The mayor was thus not only a powerful figure in the local administration, but one whose claim to represent the whole of the local community served to suppress the expression of local political conflicts (see also Kesselman 1970). Similarly, in order for the mayor to enhance his status, he sought to cultivate close relationships with the *préfet* who gave the mayor the appearance of having, as it were, a friend at court in the Ministry of the Interior. The *préfet* and the mayor thus developed a common set of interests which were sometimes opposed to those of the Ministry of the Interior, as well as of other central ministries in Paris.

From this model of interdependence, a whole body of work, associated with Michel Crozier's *Groupe de Sociologie des Organisations*, emerged to confirm this basic model of interdependence and elaborate upon it (Grémion, P. 1970, 1976; Crozier and Thoenig 1976; Thoenig 1978 are examples). These showed an interpenetration between central and local government which constrained the scope of independent action by both central and local political and administrative actors. The patterns of interdependence prevailing in the urban areas differed somewhat from the pattern found in the rural areas on which Worms' (1966) study was based (see Thoenig 1978, and Schain 1981, for example). In particular, the larger cities gained a more direct access to central processes of decision-making through the *cumul des mandats*, the practice of acquiring several elected officers at the same time (mayor, departmental councillor, regional councillor and member of the National Assembly), and thus strengthening an individual's influence in the French politico-administrative system (see Becquart-Leclercq 1978). Given this relationship of interdependence between central and local government, it has been impossible for central government to take unilateral policy initiatives without either negotiating with, or anticipating the reactions of, local government actors (Ashford 1982).

In 1982, the Mitterrand government started the process of legislating a whole package of decentralisation reforms. So far the most important consequence of the reforms has been the transmutation of the *préfet* into a Commissioner of the Republic (*Commissionaire de la République*) and the transfer of greater powers to the departmental councils, *Conseils Généraux* (see Hayward 1983: 28–9). The precise significance of these reforms cannot be evaluated at present (but see Mabileau 1983; Mény 1983). However, for our purposes the conclusions are clear—the tutelage model does not accurately describe the relationship between central and local government and the interdependence of central and local political and administrative actors, and the interpenetration of central and local politics means that the centre cannot be said to 'control' the 36,000 *communes* of the French local government system.

The British position is somewhat different. In the 1970s the characterisation of British local government as the mere 'agent' of central government (Hartley 1971) came under criticism from a variety of scholars. Above all, Boaden's (1971) path-breaking study of variations in local government expenditure showed that local authorities derived their own expenditure priorities without these being strictly defined by central government; and Dearlove (1973) showed that local government policy-making appeared relatively unconstrained by any form of central government intervention. In the late 1970s, alternatives to the 'agent' model became very popular among British academics (see Rhodes 1981), and the most popular of these models bore strong similarities to those used to describe centre–periphery relations in France and the United States. According to this model (Rhodes 1981), local and central government were interdependent, not least because local government required central government statutes and money to be able to provide local services; and central government depended upon local government to deliver a substantial portion of state services. Local government had resources which it could use to bargain with central government in this relationship of interdependence—it had among other things the legitimacy afforded through public election and a variety of statutory rights, including that of raising its own revenue through local rates and charges. The bargaining between central and local government takes place largely between the national interest groups (see Rhodes 1983) composed of local government councillors, such as the Association of County Councils and the Association of Metropolitan Authorities, as well as groups of council officials, such as the Chartered Institute of Public Finance and Accountancy and the Society of Local Authority Chief Executives. This contrasts with the direct relationships between the centre and individual authorities in France (see Kesselman 1970). The system of bargaining is a complex one, a complexity compounded by the fact that different arrangements for bargaining could be found between the distinctive central and local government organisations in Scotland, England, Wales and Northern Ireland (see Page 1980; Rose 1982). From this pattern of complexity and bargaining it could be concluded that 'ostensibly hierarchical relationships dissolve under the exigencies of implementing a policy' (Rhodes 1981: 26).

The actions, first of the 1974 Labour government following the onset of fiscal stringency in the mid-1970s, and then of the Conservative government since 1979 have, however, shown that central government has the capacity and will to take unilateral decisions without giving much away in bargaining with local authority groups. It can make issues non-negotiable. Central government has mandated the sale of council houses, cut grants, restructured the grant system and introduced legislation to limit the traditional freedom of local authorities to determine the level of rate they levy, all in the face of the most vocal opposition from local authorities and their associations. Doubtless, many issues in central–local relations, from the drafting of model bye-laws to the preparation of legislation for local authorities' involvement in treating the mentally handicapped, remain subjects for negotiation and bargaining in the manner suggested by the bargaining framework. Yet the actions of the central government in policy areas which it regards as key ones show that, in Britain unlike France, there are relatively few constraints on central government using its constitutional superiority to seek to secure the policy outcomes it desires.

One of the main reasons for this is the traditional separation between national and local politics (Ashford 1982; Bulpitt 1983). While in France the interpenetration of national and local politics serves to limit the ability of the national level to take unilateral decisions, in Britain there is a relatively clear separation between national and local politicians. British MPs rarely perceive themselves to be major defenders of the interests of their locality and any individual contact between central government and a single local authority generally takes place via the local government officials rather than local politicians (Griffith 1966). While Britain has traditionally been regarded as the international example of 'local self-government' (von Gneist 1891), British local self-government has been based upon the granting of a wide range of functions and broad discretion to local authorities, with relatively little direct interaction between individual local politicians and national government departments and politicians. The political pressures that local government actors have exerted on central government via the national associations which the centre has chosen to ignore on many crucial issues are relatively weak. When central government wishes to limit these broad discretionary powers of local authorities, or even change the functions that they fulfil or reorganise them, there are no powerful mechanisms, such as can be found in France, to enable local government to influence the centre. The importance of these powerful influences in France and their absence in Britain is seen particularly clearly in the case of the process of local government reform in the 1970s (see Ashford 1982).

The German system of intergovernmental relations which, according to the formal constitutional rules, sees the federal government as having general directive competences for a large number of state and local functions, has also been subject to criticism. The most elaborate study of the German federal system, by Scharpf, Reissert and Schnabel (1976) postulates a model of 'policy interpenetration' (*Politikverflechtung*) which, resulting from the interdependence of different levels of government, is, of course, envisaged in the constitutional provisions of the Bonn Republic, with its emphasis upon hierarchical rather than functional divisions of competences between different levels of government. However, the constitutional model of a hierarchy as between federal, state and local government does not correspond to reality. Rather, the interdependence and interpenetration of federal, state and local government has produced a system in which policies are developed within the intergovernmental system so as to maximise consensus between the different actors and institutions involved in them. The importance of the states in federal policy-making is also reinforced by the fact that the consent of the states through the *Bundesrat* is required for policies which affect state and local government (Ziller 1974). Thus, for example, federal grants for particular programmes are not distributed according to any federally-defined incidence of the needs of any particular area; they are distributed on the basis of 'fair shares all round', rather than targeted according to federal priorities. The attempt to minimise conflict within the system also brings with it the fragmentation of policy-making as the different actors in the system try to separate the contentious from the non-contentious issues. Above all, the quest for consensus results in the inability of the federal government to have any clear leadership role in policy development (*Steuereungsbedarf*), even in the restricted sense envisaged in the constitution. Scharpf, Reissert and Schnabel document this extensively in a range of case studies of joint tasks or areas in which the federal government has assumed some financial responsibility: regional policy, agricultural policy, transport policy, urban development, housing and hospital finance.

The inability to exert hierarchical authority within a system of policy interpenetration is also shown in the case of state–local government relationships in the study of Baestlein *et al.* (1978) of location programmes (*Standortprogramme*) in Nordrhein-Westfalen. Local authorities in this *Land* were requested to present their plans for land use and the development of public works so that these plans could be integrated into a more comprehensive development plan for the whole *Land*. The *Land* did not have the statutory power to do this, but it indicated that financial aid from the *Land* to local authorities was conditional on the localities having submitted and received approval for their plans. What followed was an erratic stream of rather diverse plans. Despite the apparently powerful threat of withholding funds, localities, especially the larger and, from the perspective of the aims of the planning process, more important ones, did not feel compelled to follow the *Land's* injunctions:

The cities knew very well that the *Land* government could hardly afford to withhold all the financial aid to any one of them, let alone several. Experience told them that whatever came down the administrative chain of command was not always the last word, but might be altered by the political channel—if the mayor picked up the 'phone and talked to the [*Land*] minister himself (Baestlein *et al.* 1978: 139).

Similar to the French system, both at administrative and party political levels (Bertram 1967), the network of contacts between national, state and local officials, and the primacy of consensus-building among them, makes it impossible to talk simply of federal domination of the state and local government system.

In France and Germany, and to a lesser extent Britain, the accuracy of the formal constitutional description of the relationship between national and sub-national government can be questioned on the grounds that the central government does not have as much control over the actions of sub-national government as the formal constitutional principles suggest. In the United States, the criticism of the formal description suggests the opposite: that the federal role of the government of states and localities is not as limited as the 'separate authority' model of the constitution suggests. The federal government has, since the late nineteenth century (Elazar 1962), and especially following the New Deal era of the 1930s, increased its influence in state and local government policy-making, primarily through the use of federal grants in aid (see Derthick 1970). While there is no general constitutional ability for the federal government to legislate details of how state and local governments should fulfil their functions (although federal courts do have the ability to mandate), some actions may be mandated by federal legislation (see ACIR 1981c: 18), especially in the field of the environment (e.g. the Clean Air Amendments 1970) and employment (e.g. the Equal Opportunities Act 1972). More importantly, the federal government can make receipt of federal grants conditional upon the recipient states and localities meeting certain requirements; grants can have strings attached to them. The complexity of the US intergovernmental financial system does, however, allow for experienced state and local officials to avoid the conditions while receiving the grant. Moreover the prevalence of the phenomenon of 'grantsmanship', the entrepreneurial ability to use the complex system of grant aid to get federal money for one's own individual state or locality (see Hanus 1981; Wright, D.S. 1978), and the principle of 'fungibility' (referring to the ability to use federal money for purposes other than those of which it was intended), mean that one cannot simply equate federal grants with direct supervision and control of state and local government. Rather, it is the fact that grant aid programmes bring federal, state and local administrators and politicians together to *negotiate* levels of grant, the conditions attached to them, and the degree to which a state or locality is conforming with the conditions rather than the conditions alone that gives the federal government influence in the intergovernmental system of the United States (see Derthick 1970; Beer 1973, 1977; Ingram 1977).

Instead of federal–state–local relations being conceived of as a 'layer cake' of separate authority, the development of the intergovernmental system, in particular through the development of the intergovernmental grant system, has come to resemble, in Grodzins' (1960) famous phrase, a 'marble cake' in which the uneven and complex pattern of the different layers represents the intermingling of responsibilities between different levels of government. Another of the graphic analogies used to describe the US system of intergovernmental relations is that of 'picket fence' federalism (see Wright, D.S. 1978: 61–3). This refers to the vertical as opposed to the horizontal structuring of the intergovernmental system in which the major actors in the system are identified by their functional concerns (highways, welfare, education, hospitals, housing, for example), rather than their institutional affiliation to either federal, state or local government. A federal official in the education sector has more in common with his counterpart at state and local level than with federal officials in other policy areas. These common values among federal, state and local officials make it all the more difficult to isolate precisely where policy initiatives tend to originate in the federal system.

The development of the federal grant system has often been characterised as a centralisation of US federalism. It has even been taken to suggest that the US system is developing towards a system which is federal in name only, with the federal government assuming the type of directive control frequently assumed to be characteristic of unitary states (Lowi 1979: 49–50). This picture is an inaccurate one, not only because it makes unwarranted assumptions about the nature of central government control in unitary states, but also because while the influence of the federal government in the federal system has undoubtedly increased, especially since the New Deal era, federal influence remains *influence* and not *control* in a complex system in which the scope for avoiding unwanted federal influence while receiving wanted federal funds is substantial (see Hanus 1981).

CONCLUSION

If there exists a *Beamtenherrschaft* (dominance by officials) in any of the four countries of this study, then it is not that form of *Beamtenherrschaft* suggested by the writings of élite theorists, that is to say, of a small, cohesive élite group running the machinery of government. Government organisations are too fragmented for this to be the case. At central or federal government level there is a variety of different organisations which operate largely independently of one another, and even where central or federal government does seek to assert particular policy priorities, it is by no means certain that these will be carried out in areas for which state and local governments have competences.

If there are any distinctions to be drawn between the degree to which the hierarchical structure pervades the four countries, then the most obvious distinction to be drawn is the one that exists between the US organisation of government and the European organisation of government. While the number of organisations and their complexity does not distinguish between Britain and other European polities and the United States, as Rose (1980b) points out the United States lacks the integrative mechanisms found in European nations such as a central and powerful Treasury or Finance Ministry as well as, in Britain, a strong service-wide civil service ethos. One must be careful not to overstate the degree to which European nations are characterised in such a way, since, for example, the *Bundesbank* in West Germany has acted independently to impose constraints upon German government (Dyson 1982a). Yet in the European nations there exist stronger factors producing a focus for cohesion, not a single pyramid-style organisation, than are found in the United States.

If one is looking for spatial analogies, executive organisation in each of the four countries is more accurately characterised as a mountain range than a single pyramid. The implications of this fragmentation within government is that *if* the administrative apparatus were found to be immune from political pressures from outside—from parliament, interest groups or political leaders—then the type of *Beamtenherrschaft* that we might expect conforms more closely to the type that emerges from the satrapic conflicts of a fragmented administrative system: policies and decisions emerge from a processing of conflicts within a far from cohesive administrative apparatus without any scope for political direction (see also Peters 1981).

However, consideration of the internal properties of the administrative systems of the four countries limits only the type of *Beamtenherrschaft* we might expect. It tells us little about the actual limitations which the administrative system imposes upon the exercise of political leadership in the four countries. The scope for political leadership within a bureaucratic system of government depends also upon the influences exerted upon the administrative system from those who are not permanent officials: legislators, interest groups, courts, ministers, and their advisers. It is to the relationship between the administrative system and these groups that the remainder of this book is devoted.

4   Parliament in a Bureaucracy

That Weber did not regard the dominance by officials (*Beamtenherrschaft*) as inevitable has already been discussed; that he saw the development of parliament, at least before the founding of the Weimar Republic, as one of the main vehicles for the prevention of the dominance of officials needs some discussion since Weber is not conventionally associated with theories of parliamentary government: in fact, parliamentary government receives little prominence within his discussion of ideal types. Rather, it is quite extensively elaborated in the context of his penetrating analyses of the condition of politics in Imperial Germany. Many of the statements about the role of parliament are specifically derived from the conditions prevailing in the early years of the twentieth century in Germany, and Weber's own emphasis upon parliamentary government undoubtedly reflects his concern with establishing a parliamentary system in Germany after the end of the first world war. (For a discussion of Weber's role in the creation of the institutions of the Weimar Republic, see Meyer 1964). However, it is possible to derive some general principles from his writings about the role of parliament in a bureaucratic system of government.

Weber (1972: 851) argues that parliaments are the outward sign of the 'minimum of internal consent' required within a bureaucratic form of government from the citizens it rules (or at least on the part of the 'most important social classes'). At a minimum, parliaments fulfil some form of validating or ratifying role with respect to the proposals passed on to it by the executive: i.e. giving assent to Bills for laws or budgetary proposals. This requirement that many executive actions require parliamentary assent is indeed important, but ultimately limited,

> As long as a parliament can only express popular disaffection with the administration through refusing to give consent to budgetary of legislative proposals . . . then it is excluded from any positive participation in political leadership. It will only be able to engage in 'negative politics', that is to say, it will confront the leadership of the administration as an enemy power, be given only the minimum of information by it and be regarded as an encumbrance by the executive. (Weber 1972: 851)

Weber contrasted the rather minor, negative role that parliament could play—and actually played rather poorly in Imperial Germany—with the more positive form of parliamentary government in which 'a working government continually collaborates with the administration and controls it' (Weber 1972: 854). The positive influence is achieved partly by the *Enquêterecht* (the right of scrutiny) that parliament has over the executive. This itself has two main components: the first lies in the generation of information about the executive (*Verwaltungsöffentlichkeit*). Since bureaucratic rule is rule on the basis of knowledge, publication of the actions of government is a precondition for any sort of wider participation in that rule. Furthermore, Weber argues that secrecy is the most important source of power for permanent officials, and therefore its erosion through parliamentary scrutiny serves as a check on the dominance by officials.

The second component was the collaboration it brought with the executive departments. Weber argued that it was not enough (and indeed probably not a good idea in view of the work load) for a parliament to produce voluminous reports exhaustively documenting received evidence and deliberations concerning the performance of executive departments. Rather, scrutiny had to be directed towards the establishment of a close working relationship with executive departments, through contacts with permanent officials as well as ministers. It is for this reason that Weber (1972: 855) stresses the 'continual *collaboration* and influence upon the direction of the administration' and the attempt to compel the 'leader of the administration to enter into a dialogue' with parliament, making the actual use of the legal right of enquiry superfluous. Without such routinised collaboration, Weber argued, the right of scrutiny would degenerate into confrontational modes of relationship which limit parliament to a negative role, as he argued was the case in Italy and France in the early twentieth century.

Apart from the right of scrutiny, Weber argued that parliaments could have a second important role, that of selecting and training political leaders—that group of people which emerged along with the development of bureaucratic forms of government. As discussed in Chapter 2, for Weber (1958: 335) the essence of political leadership is 'struggle, the building of coalitions and popularity'. This involved in part developing the qualities of the demagogue. Now it did not matter much that members of parliament were not particularly assertive *vis à vis* the executive; Weber argued that British MPs were 'no more than well-disciplined lobby fodder [*gut diszipliniertes Stimmvieh*]' due to the development of party cohesion. It was the training within the party and parliament, struggling for power, constructing coalitions and building up a following (*freie Gefolgschaft*), that offered the training for this form of demagoguery. However, a properly functioning parliament, Weber argued, offered more than this. It allowed those versed in the skills of demagoguery to develop a sense of the realities of government operations (see Weber 1958: 342–3) and produced political leaders capable of leading the administrative system as ministers, not 'mere demagogues'. Of course, this is a role that the US Congress cannot fulfill (see Weber 1958: 385) since heads of executive organisations cannot be members of Congress, although the similar position of parliament in France's Fifth Republic has not prevented the French parliament from making an important contribution to the careers of members of the executive (see below).

Consequently, there are four dimensions to be explored concerning the role of parliaments in a bureaucratic system. First, there is the degree to which parliament fulfils what Weber argued to be a 'negative' approach of approving legislation. Second, there is the control of the executive (similarly assumed to be a negative control) through the need to ratify public spending decisions taken by the executive. Third, there is the positive role of actually collaborating with and influencing the administration through dialogue and scrutiny. And fourth, there is the role of parliament as the arena for the recruitment of political leaders. The focus of this examination will be the West German *Bundestag*, both Houses of the US Congress, the French *Assemblée Nationale*, and the British House of Commons. (For a discussion of the role of the House of Lords, see Norton 1981; of the *Bundesrat*, see Ziller 1974; and of the *Sénat*, see Mastias 1980.)

LEGISLATION: A NEGATIVE POWER?

It was a common cliché in the 1960s that legislatures were everywhere in decline. One of the reasons for arguing this was that legislatures appeared to have a rather limited role in legislating. This is not primarily because legislatures can be by-passed in the process of legislation, although in each of the four countries it is possible to by-pass the legislature and pass laws in the form of decrees, statutory instruments or executive orders (see Rose 1983). Rather, such arguments pointed to the limited role of parliaments in the actual passage of legislation which appeared to be confined to approving the legislative proposals of the executive and making only minute textual amendments to them. Even the United States Congress, traditionally regarded as the most powerful of legislatures, was perceived to be in decline in the 1960s with the President as 'chief legislator' (Sundquist 1981).

The evidence as concerns the initiation of legislation certainly bears this out in France, West Germany and Britain, since most successful legislation originates in the executive. In France 87 per cent of the legislation reaching the statute book in the first twenty years of the Fifth Republic came from the executive, while the equivalent figure for Britain was only slightly lower at 82 per cent

(Frears 1981). In Germany, the figure is somewhat lower again at 78 per cent (von Beyme 1983). Moreover, the precise dimensions of executive dominance are difficult to gauge because some private members' legislation is effectively sponsored by the executive. This dominance of the executive over the initiation of legislation can be explained in part by the fact that party discipline in each legislature produces a heavy bias towards the adoption of government legislation, as well as by the limitations within each of the three countries on the time that may be devoted to private members' legislation. In addition, in France there are constitutional limitations placed upon the content of private members' legislation which mean that no private legislation can increase expenditure or decrease revenue (see Hayward 1983).

If the role of parliament in the legislative process in each of the three countries were to be judged on the basis of the degree to which legislation is initiated by individual members of parliament, then the role of parliament would indeed be a negative one—that of refusing to pass legislative initiatives; furthermore, it would be one which the legislatures do not exercise to any great degree. The success rate of executive proposed legislative initiatives is 73 per cent in Germany (Rausch 1976: 126); in France this was 72 per cent; and Britain 93 per cent (Rose 1983: 11), with those executive-proposed laws not reaching the statute book rarely failing due to outright defeat in parliament.

Of course, the role of parliament in legislation is not solely limited to initiating legislation: parliaments also have the power to amend legislative proposals. Perhaps the greatest divergence between the three European countries is found here. In Britain, amendments are usually proposed during the passage of the legislation through a standing committee (see Norton 1981, for a discussion of legislative procedures). The role of the individual member is again rather limited, primarily due to the pressures of party discipline as well as the nature of the exercise: a detailed look at the text of the legislation without any opportunity to question witnesses about the reasoning behind it. It is for this reason that Richard Crossman, as Minister of Housing and Local

Government, complained about the 'insane' mode of working of the standing committees which went line-by-line through legislation that nobody understood, with government and opposition members reading out their briefs from either the ministry or pressure groups, with no 'genuine committee work' of examining witnesses and discussing the broad principles of the policy at stake (see Griffith 1977). Backbenchers' amendments have a success rate of under 5 per cent, while those moved by the government have a success rate approaching 100 per cent (Griffith 1974: 93). While the percentages changed in the 1974–9 period of a Labour minority government in favour of the private member (see Schwarz 1980; Norton 1981), the dominance of the executive in the legislative process is clear and persistent (see Walkland 1968).

The French legislature is traditionally regarded as subordinate to the executive (see Wright, V. 1978), but the committee work of the French parliament, through the *Commissions Permanentes* in the Assembly and the Senate, appears to offer greater scope for amending executive proposals than those found in Britain. These committees have the ability to question ministers and civil servants, although they have no right to compel attendance, and hearings involving senior officials and ministers are usually conducted *in camera* (see Loquet 1981). Amendments proposed by the executive still have a very high chance of success (81 per cent), yet amendments proposed from members of the *Commissions Permanentes* are also frequently sustained (66 per cent), indicating a more active role for French MPs than their British counterparts in amending legislation. Neither are the amendments proposed by members of parliament always trivial. Frears (1981: 61) cites two examples of amendments introduced at committee stage: the changes in 1977 that communist members managed to make concerning the time period for eligibility for social security benefits, and the socialist and communist success later that year in lengthening the expiry period of guarantees given to work completed by firms in the construction industry.

German committees, the main bodies for amending

legislation, commonly enjoy a greater reputation for amending government legislation than their British and French
counterparts (see King 1976). While there are no statistics
available comparable to those given in France and Britain,
Lohmar's evidence (cited in Rausch 1976: 125), based on
the working of three committees over the period 1971–4,
appears to back up this reputation; 45 per cent of Bills
referred to them fell into Lohmar's category of 'substantially' amended, i.e. were subject to a large quantity of
amendments relative to the length of the legislation.
However, as Johnson (1979: 131) points out, the activism of
the *Bundestag* committees in amending legislation should
not be interpreted as indicating executive weakness since
much of the activity of the committees is concerned with
detailed and often exhaustive discussion of the *sachlich*
(factual) features which dominate most items of proposed
legislation; that is to say, most of the discussion and
amending concerns items of technical detail rather than the
broad outlines of the policy contained in the legislative
proposals. This leads Johnson (1979: 131) to comment that
'governments are now rarely defeated, and initiatives from
their opponents have practically no chance of success
without government tolerance and support'. While German
committees have greater powers of calling evidence and
conventionally scrutinise legislation in great detail, the
committees in Germany share with those in Britain and
France a limited power of amendment within an executive–
dominated legislative process.

The United States legislative system contrasts strongly
with those of the three European nations. Certainly, the
influence of Congress is a variable rather than a constant.
For example, it has been argued (see Sundquist 1981: 127–
54) that the traditional predominance of the legislative
branch in law-making was eroded in the early decades of the
twentieth century and especially during the New Deal era, in
which the President 'emerged as chief legislator', and 'by the
mid-1960s . . . most scholars conceded that the legislative
initiative had passed from Congress to the President'
(Sundquist 1981: 148). As Moe and Teel (1970) point out,
many of the discussions which suggested that the US

Congress had developed towards a British model of an executive-dominated legislature were based on an under-estimation of the precise degree to which Congress initiated and amended legislation. Yet, however severe one evaluates the decline of Congress to have been, and however impressive its resurgence (Sundquist 1981), the central point for a comparative evaluation is that in contrast to the European nations, Congress is responsible for the bulk of successful legislative initiatives—90 per cent (Rose 1983: 11). Many of the major initiatives in the expansion of government activities can be attributed to the actions of individual zealot members of Congress (ACIR 1981b) and the President's own policy initiatives have, in comparison with the European nations, a low chance of success in Congress, with Rose (1983: 11) indicating a success rate for the President's legislative proposals of only 30 per cent.

It is not possible to give a detailed account of the interaction between the legislature and the executive in law-making. (For a good discussion of legislation–executive relations in comparative perspective; see King 1976; Mezey 1979). Undoubtedly, the role of parliament in legislation is not fully appreciated through examination of the formal procedures alone; for example, the anticipated reactions of members of parliament may be regarded as a form of influence upon the legislative process (see, for example, Norton 1981). As Johnson (1979: 135) points out in the German case, a government might react to parliamentary pressure by sponsoring amendments to its own legislation which largely preserve the character of the legislation, rather than seek to enforce party discipline. However, in terms of the initiation of legislation, the role of parliament in the European countries is, especially in comparison with the US Congress, relatively slight. In the European countries, the executive dominates the parliamentary timetable and has a very high chance of its measures reaching the statute book. Certainly, the amendment of legislation is not entirely a negative power, at least not in France and Germany, where committees are far more likely to amend legislation than they are in Britain. Nevertheless, in these three countries it is still the executive which dominates the legislature. The executive has a high chance of securing the amendments that it wants, and overturning the executive in committee on a key issue is still enough of a rarity to distinguish the European legislatures from the American. This distinction conforms to Mezey's (1979: 36) characterisation of the European legislatures as 'reactive' in contrast to the 'active' US Congress. Any broad characterisation of legislative–executive relations must be qualified by the recognition that statements about legislative strength and weakness refer are a matter of degree. Some parliamentary legislative initiatives can succeed. Parliaments have made important amendments to executive legislation, and the influence of legislatures may vary within each country over time (see the important increase in the role of the House of Commons in the 1970s in Schwarz 1980; Norton 1981). However, the European experience, but certainly not the American, largely conforms to Weber's expectation of a negative role for legislatures in legislation.

BUDGETARY CONTROL

Budgets are typically the product of a complex bargaining relationship within the executive (see Lord 1972; Wildavsky 1974; Mayntz and Scharpf 1975; Heclo and Wildavsky 1981; Hayward 1983). Budgets are not, of course, made *de novo* each year. Government programmes are frequently defined by law, and many of these, such as the so-called 'uncontrollables' in the United States (including social security payments), are based on statutory commitments to expenditure which cannot be altered within the budgetary process alone. Furthermore, the process of budgeting is largely *incremental* (see Wildavsky 1974), that is to say, based on the acceptance of the previous year's budget as the basis for drawing up that of the following year. With some exceptions, such as with the fate of capital expenditure for British local authorities in the late 1970s and early 1980s (see Rose and Page 1982), the political conflict and bargaining about expenditure levels for particular departments and programmes is concerned with changes at the *margin* over previous budgetary allocations.

(For a recent discussion, see Dempster and Wildavsky 1979.) Since the end of the period of 'treble affluence' (Rose and Peters 1978), with rising gross national product, rising take-home pay and rising public expenditure in the middle of the 1970s, these margins have been negative as well as positive. The role of legislatures in budgetary decisions shows up once again the difference between the US Congress on the one hand, and the parliaments of West Germany, France and Britain on the other.

In Britain the planned total of public expenditure and its distribution result from the political process of bargaining involving the Cabinet, individual spending departments and the Treasury—often known as the PESC process after the name of the interdepartmental committee of civil servants, the Public Expenditure Survey Committee, which is responsible for providing an assessment of the likely future costs of existing policy commitments. (For accounts of this process, see Pliatzky 1980; Barnett 1981; Copeman 1981; Heclo and Wildavsky 1981). Parliament only gets involved following publication of the fruits of this process in the government's White Paper, usually entitled *The Government's Expenditure Plans*, in a debate on the White Paper, and in the debate on the actual supply estimates derived from the PESC process. The debates do not produce any changes in the spending decisions. Even in 1977, when the minority Labour government was defeated in the debate on the White Paper, it managed to save itself and its public expenditure plans by turning the issue into a vote of confidence and forming an alliance with the Liberal Party to win it. The twenty-nine supply days which were formally designed for debate of the supply estimates were rarely used for that purpose. Changes introduced in the 1982–3 season, including the replacement of the twenty-nine supply days with nineteen 'opposition' days plus the introduction of three 'estimates' days and the creation of the National Audit Office (Drewry 1983), may well have improved the quality of Commons public spending scrutiny, yet they have not altered the fact that parliament is at most only peripherally involved in public spending decisions in Britain (Brazier 1983). While there are scrutiny committees in parliament,

notably the Public Accounts Committee (Flegman 1980) and
the Select Committee on the Treasury and Civil Service (and
formerly the Expenditure Committee abolished in 1979),
parliament impinges little on the actual process of budgeting. The Study of Parliament Group (1980: 40) sums up the
weakness of the role of the British Parliament in public
expenditure decisions:

The general lack of positive response by governments to the work
of the Expenditure Committee, the poor attendances at some
expenditure related debates, and the general lack of interest in the
details of expenditure all indicate that the influence of the House
of Commons, through its formal procedures, is limited.

Similarly in France, the budgetary process is largely
internal to the executive, with the budget itself reflecting a
process of bargaining between the finance ministry, the
individual ministries, the *Conseil des Ministres* and the
President (see Lord 1972; Green 1981). While the budget is
formally passed to parliament as a proposed law and is
debated, the 'ensuing consideration of the budget by
parliament in the autumn rarely brings . . . [the] general
decisions into question' (Groupe des Spécialistes des Études
Parlementaires 1980: 129). This role is further constrained
by the constitutional limitations upon the changes which
parliament may make to the Finance Bill—it is not permitted, according to Article 40 of the 1958 constitution, to vote
increases in the budget without the acceptance of the
executive. Furthermore, the budget as debated has only a
loose relationship to the actual amount of money that the
government spends, since the totals discussed reflect ceiling
levels of expenditure and the departments might not always
draw upon their full allocation. In addition, extra money
may be required in the form of supplementary estimates,
and parliament rarely debates these. It is even possible for
the government to raise extra sums of money without
parliamentary consent using its own statutory powers (see
Groupe des Spécialistes des Études Parlementaires 1980:
129). However, despite the formal limitations, it is custom-
ary for the parliamentary discussion of the budget to commit

the government to slightly more expenditure than stated in the formal submission. Indeed, the practice of the government accepting amendments as a minor concession to deputies is well established. The executive is primarily concerned that its budget

should pass quickly and unscathed through parliament by the end of December. . . . Provided it is willing to set aside about 0.05 per cent of the budget to make a number of minor but politically popular concessions to its own parliamentary supporters, the government can secure the legitimation of its budget by parliament. Finance ministers deliberately make provision for such concessions that allow deputies to boast of their victories at his expense. (Hayward 1983: 194)

One major difference between Germany and the other two European nations in this study in the parliamentary role in the budgetary process is in the fact that the German parliament, by means of the *Haushaltsausschuss* (the budget committee) is consulted prior to the formal submission of the budget to parliament (Rausch 1976: 110). The detailed discussion of the budget offers members the chance of examining more areas of government policy outside budgetary policy. Ellwein (1973: 291) discusses how the budget allows the *Bundestag* to 'get involved in personnel issues and hinder the promotion of a civil servant and influence road building'. Constitutionally, the *Bundestag* is limited in the degree to which it can make changes to the budget by Article 113 of the Basic Law, which requires executive approval for increases in expenditure. However, there have been occasions when the budget has been substantively amended in the *Bundestag*, such as in 1965 when 2.5bn Deutschmarks were added to the federal budget. However, it is rare for the *Bundestag* to make major changes to the budget, especially since the introduction of multi-year targets for public expenditure in 1967 (Ellwein 1973: 291), which leads Ellwein to conclude that the *Bundestag* might use the budgetary scrutiny role to influence the development of policy in a number of detailed areas, 'but it does not make budgetary policy; this function remains with the government.'

Thus, in each of the three European nations, the role of parliament in budgetary decisions is essentially a rather limited one. Like its legislative role, it reacts to initiatives taken by the executive, and the politics of the budgetary process is largely a set of conflicts and compromises between members of the executive. In the United States, the position is different. The traditional power of the US congressional committees in the budgetary process was summarised by the observation that the 'United States . . . does not have a fiscal policy, it has a fiscal result' (Sundquist 1981: 199–200). The President's programme, once it emerged from the process of bargaining within the executive branch involving the White House, largely through the Office of Management and Budget (see Berman 1979), and the executive agencies (see Wildavsky 1974), was pulled apart once it arrived in Congress. Taxation issues were separated from spending issues: spending issues were assigned to a variety of separate appropriations sub-committees, with substantive committees themselves having the power to pass legislation committing federal funds whether they were envisaged in the budget or not (see Thurber 1981). As Caiden (1982: 518) points out, the doctrine of the separation of powers prevented executive domination of the budgetary process: 'unfortunately neither this nor any other doctrine provided any compensatory machinery to reconcile deadlocks between the executive and legislature or enforce consistent budgeting policies on congress.' The 1974 Congressional Budget and Impoundment Control Act sought to introduce a greater degree of coherence to the congressional role in the budgetary process through setting-up procedures which sought to make Congress think about the budget as a whole consisting of interrelated parts. (For a dicsussion of the background, see Schick 1981; Sundquist 1981; Hartman 1982). The idea was that the new House and Senate budget committees would receive the budgetary proposals from the President and report to Congress which would pass a first concurrent resolution in May providing guidelines for committees and sub-committees in the detailed discussion of the budget. Before the first resolution, legislation authorising new expenditure should have been passed. After the budget had been dealt with by the appropriations committees and sub-committees, the budget committee would prepare a second resolution to be passed by Congress (in September), revising the estimates of the first. Thereafter there would be a process of reconciliation of the appropriations and authorisations with the second resolution.

The early years of this process saw little change from the pre-existing model of the congressional role in budgeting. Above all, the initial budget resolution was largely ignored in the subsequent committee and sub-committee work. Committees authorising expenditure did not stick to the timetable, and there was still the major problem of 'uncontrollable' spending, the major programmes covering entitlements, such as welfare benefits which are outside the purview of the annual budgetary cycle (see Caiden 1982). Carter, and especially Reagan, tried to strengthen the executive influence on the budgetary process in Congress by using the *first* budget resolution as the basis for reconciliation with the commitments emanating from the committees and sub-committees. This was used in 1981 (for the 1982 budget) to achieve major reductions in expediture. However, that this strategy is limited is underlined by the fact that Members of Congress were disturbed about the consequences of this strategy and were unlikely to acquiesce in it again.

The experience of the 1982 budget prejudiced the following year's budgetary process in advance. . . . Reconciliation, despite its success in achieving the administration's policy goals, had been seen by many as dictatorial because it pushed literally hundreds of measures through Congress virtually without debate. (Caiden 1982: 51).

Few commentators envisaged that the President could maintain the degree of influence that he had in the 1982 budget. Caiden (1982) saw signs of the breaking-up of the budgetary process following the 1982 budget. This was, she argued, the 'logical accumulation of past trends'. While the success of the Reagan administration in achieving cuts cannot be denied, and while in addition the 1974 Congressional Budget and Impoundment Control Act brought major changes in the congressional budgetary process, the process is far from under the control of the executive as one could describe the process in the three Western European states.

One must, of course, be cautious when seeking to ascribe 'control' to public expenditure in any country (Wright, M. 1977), since many items of expenditure are either impossible (debt charges) or extremely difficult (social security payments) to change from one year to the next. Furthermore, as incremental budgeting theory informs us (Wildavsky 1974), budgeting is incremental, with the bulk of expenditure, the base, rarely being questioned from one year to the next. As such, political bargaining and negotiation conventionally involve discussion of margins of increase or decrease from previous years' spending, rather than of the base. It is in this context that one talks of the role of the legislature in the budgetary process. In the European nations the role of the legislatures is relatively peripheral, with negotiation and bargaining surrounding margins of expenditure decrease, and increase largely involving the executive alone. It is this which allows one to argue that, in contrast to the United States, in so far as anyone controls the budget in the European states, it is the executive.

LEGISLATIVE SCRUTINY

The term 'scrutiny', in addition to how it can be assessed in the context of legislative–executive relations, is open to different interpretations. There is some ambiguity over the question of whether scrutiny should be exercised before the fact, after the fact, or both (see Aberbach 1979; Sundquist 1981). In the context of this analysis there are two major concerns about the functioning of scrutiny by legislatures, conceived of here as the involvement of groups within the legislature in the development of policy outside the legislative process. First, consistent with the publicity function discussed above, it is necessary to know whether legislatures have the ability to learn and publish details about the workings of government departments and agencies, and how policy is developed within them. Secondly, it is necessary to know how far legislatures—or more usually the committees within them—are institutions with which the executive branch, and above all the permanent officials within it, feels it must establish a routine dialogue. How far does the executive perceive that issues should be routinely 'cleared' by members of the legislature, and how far are representatives in parliament kept informed of policy developments within executive departments and agencies?

In Britain, the main potential arenas for the development of more routine contacts between the legislature and the executive departments are the specialist committees such as the Public Accounts Committee (see Flegman 1980) and the select committees. Looking at the select committees (of which fourteen were set up in 1979, although they share common characteristics with pre-existing committees; see Johnson 1977), these undoubtedly serve the function of publicising those actions of the executive which they choose to scrutinise through their reports as well as through the publication of their evidence and hearings. There are, of course, limits to the degree to which the committees can rely upon the government departments for information, since there is no legal compulsion to submit evidence or to attend and give evidence, and some committees have in their reports complained of the reluctance of government departments to provide full and frank evidence (see Downs 1983). However, much of what we know about the current operation of government departments comes from select committee reports and evidence; as, indeed, the old generation of committees provided valuable evidence on governmental operations (see Johnson 1977). However, as with the old committees, one can doubt their actual influence upon policy-making. Certainly, there have been no spectacular successes of the new select committees in forming policy and, as Johnson (1977) points out, neither should one expect these in a system in which the executive can rely upon majority support in parliament. Whether, despite the limitations of the influence of the committees, they have managed to establish a status within Whitehall as important bodies to be kept routinely informed of the work of government ministries is as yet uncertain given that the new generation of committees is so recent. *The Economist* (14–20 August 1982) offered a picture of Whitehall officials living in constant fear of the committees and seeking to gain their approval for a wide range of their actions. The evidence for this is, however, slight. On the basis of the performance of the earlier committees, it is unlikely that these new committees will command attention in Whitehall because the persistence of the party system in parliament makes the threat of substantive opposition to government policy an empty one. Consequently, the conclusion on the British system must be, at present, that although the scrutiny committees produce valuable if sometimes limited information, they do not resemble the collaborative arrangements that Weber sets out as his definition of a working parliament.

In France and Germany, the role of committees in pursuing enquiries into executive actions and policies outside the main highway of legislation appears to be more limited than in Britain by virtue of the fact that these committees are set up on an *ad hoc* basis. However, the limitations of parliamentary scrutiny in Germany and France, especially the limitation imposed by the requirement of parliamentary support of the majority party(ies) for the government, are also shared by Britain and serve to highlight the weaknesses of the British scrutiny system.

Under the Fifth Republic, parliamentary inquiry commissions (*commissions d'enquête* and *commissions de contrôle*) can only be set up with the support of a majority in parliament. This limits, on *a priori* grounds, their scope, with only eight established in the *Assemblée* between 1958 and 1978 (Frears 1981: 67–8). Their mode of operation— they have a limited life (six months), government officials, as in Britain, are not compelled to attend or provide information, hearings are often heard *in camera*, and the results of their work rarely gains much parliamentary attention—lead Masclet (1979: 308) to comment that

The powers at the disposal of [the French] parliament are regulated in such a way as to prevent the daily surveillance of governmental activity, it is a surveillance which, it is feared, only engenders parliamentary paralysis and contributes nothing to the restoration of parliamentary omnipotence.

The system of parliamentary scrutiny committees has covered some controversial topics, such as the Dassault scandal involving the alleged misuse of public funds by an aviation company headed by a French deputy, and the issue of telephone tapping. However, they generally pose little threat to the executive since the process of setting up of the committee as well as its deliberations are dominated by the members of the majority sympathetic to the government. Frears (1981: 69) even interprets the increase in the number of scrutiny committees in the 1970s as an indicator of the fact that the government is confident that these committees are of relatively little consqeuence. Scrutiny in France produces little by way of information and does not involve parliamentarians in a close and persistent dialogue with central ministries.

In Germany, the permanent committees may also act as inquiry committees, or special investigatory committees may be set up. The constraints upon the committees of inquiry in the West German *Bundestag*, the *Untersuchungsausschüsse*, are similar to those in France. While there are greater possibilities for minority use of scrutiny committees, since only one-quarter of *Bundestag* members have to support the institution of an investigatory committee, officials can refuse to give evidence to them. The tendency for committee hearings to be conducted *in camera* has been particularly criticised since it means that

it is no control when those privy to the government are informed of secret measures under the condition that they will keep quiet about them, and are turned into mutes, made unable to exercise control by the very mechanism which is supposed to guarantee control. (Rausch 1976: 295)

There has been a tendency for the opposition parties to use the committees to embarrass the government, which underlines the problem of exercising parliamentary control in a system of party government. The logic of the supporters of the government parties was expressed clearly by the chairman of the parliamentary inquiry commission into the FIBAG housing scandal of the 1960s: 'we are hardly going to score a home goal' (quoted in Rausch 1976: 295). If there is close collaboration between members of the *Bundestag* and the executive departments, it is not produced by the specific scrutiny committees. Rather, the greater status and power of the *Bundestag* standing committees in relation to those in France and Britain are likely to produce a more persistent dialogue (Mayntz and Scharpf 1975; Johnson 1976).

While the institution of the select committees in Britain offers a more routinely available means of extracting information about the daily workings of government departments, as well as their current thinking about major policy issues, the problems of exercising a scrutiny role are similar in the three European countries. A party in parliament is unlikely to use parliamentary institutions to cause serious embarrassment to, and even less likely to impose a serious defeat upon, the government which it supports, and which claims responsibility for the workings of the executive departments. One cannot, of course, measure the degree to which legislatures fulfil a scrutiny role simply in terms of the number of times that parliament has seriously embarrassed the government. Rather, one may expect, as Weber suggested, effective scrutiny to manifest itself in close collaborative relationships between the committee and the executive organisations. However, one may postulate that a condition for some sort of effective scrutiny via such committees is the perception among the executive that the outcome of inquiries are potentially damaging to the executive department, or even the government as a whole. The limitations upon the scrutiny committees, above all the importance of parliamentary party cohesion, mean that the claim of scrutiny committees to a stake in continual and collaborative dialogue with executive departments is a weak one in the three European countries.

In the United States the limitations on the legislative scrutiny role imposed by the party system are much weaker, since parties in Congress are far less cohesive. Furthermore, their importance as influential groups in the legislative and budgetary process strengthens the potential scrutiny power of the committees and sub-committees of Congress, which may undertake scrutiny roles alongside their involvement in these processes (see Sundquist 1981: 339). Following the 1974 committee reforms (after the 1973 Bolling committee report) some committees opted to set up special separate scrutiny committees, yet the relationship between scrutiny, the granting of funds and legislation frequently remains a close one, and threat of removal of funds or changes in statutory arrangements can be used as a threat to an executive agency. Consequently, the strong position of the committees enable them to learn details concerning the operation of executive agencies, as well as ensuring that executive departments maintain a close relationship with the committees and sub-committees most closely covering their sphere of operation. One of the characteristics of a Congress in decline in the 1960s had been that it had apparently neglected its oversight function (Sundquist 1981); yet in the 1970s this use of oversight increased rapidly in quantitative terms following the Bolling committee report. In 1979, 39 per cent of all House committee hearings were devoted to oversight of the executive agencies (Sundquist 1981: 328). While there has been a substantial expansion in the quantity of oversight, a number of authors have pointed out that the quality of oversight has not increased, with oversight committees concerning themselves with 'micro-management' details of programme implementation at the expense of examining broader policy goals (Aberbach 1979; Sundquist 1981). For example, one exercise in oversight produced an 862-page report on how to improve the Department of Agriculture's administration of the food stamp scheme.

Given that much of the raw material for this examination of executive departments' activities is of necessity produced by research staff in Congress, the oversight activities of Congress lead to great resentment among senior executives who 'harried by relatively junior—often very junior—legislative employees . . . will, in the words of one of them "wonder why they ever went to work for the government"'

(Sundquist 1981: 343). Undoubtedly, the American system allows for much wider opportunities for legislative oversight of the executive branch, and it serves to reinforce the already strong forces encouraging close relationships between congressional committees and executive departments. That the consequences may not all be beneficial, with executive departments devoting an increasing amount of energy to answering the queries emanating from congressional committees and their staffs, is another matter.

PARLIAMENT AS A TRAINING GROUND FOR POLITICAL LEADERSHIP

In both Britain and Germany parliament would be expected, according to Weber, to play an important part in the recruitment of political leaders for ministerial posts because of the absence of a separation between the executive and legislative branches of government. As Weber (1958: 385) recognised, its role in the United States is negligible, with only 6 per cent of US political executives in Stanley, Mann and Doig's (1967: 41–2) study having had experience in Congress, so the US is left out of the discussion here. More complex is the position in France where the constitution which formally declares the incompatibility between electoral office and an Assembly mandate might be expected to rule out parliament as a training ground for ministers. However, Assembly members who join the government tend to 'nurse' their seats through the use of a *suppléant* (Laurens 1980: 80ff), and those without a seat usually try to find one at the earliest election following their elevation to ministerial office since 'they feel, not without justification, that a parliamentary seat gives them added political prestige and weight in negotiating with their ministerial colleagues and with their own ministries' (Wright V. 1978: 110–11). Hence, the French parliament might be expected to provide a training ground for the political leadership of ministries.

While the French system informally attaches great weight to ministers having an electoral mandate, Dogan's (1979) study shows that the major route to ministerial office in

France has developed towards what he terms 'mandarin ascent'. This refers to the tendency for ministers to possess a background as civil servants (see also Birnbaum 1982). This pattern became especially noticeable under the presidency of Valéry Giscard d'Estaing:

We can now sketch a portrait of the new kind of state secretary. He has neither party or parliamentary experience. The duties he is assigned are strictly defined. Even if he is wide-ranging, he is not asked to take a stand on general political problems. He is representative neither of a current of thought nor of a political force. He owes his appointment entirely to the confidence that the President or possibly the Prime Minister has in him. As a consequence, he is in fact responsible not to parliament, but almost exclusively to the President. He incarnates no legitimacy of his own. His position resembles that of a high civil servant who leads his service but has a political orientation and, especially important, direct relations with the political arena. (Dogan 1979: 15)

This picture bears some resemblance to that painted by Weber of the tendency in Imperial Germany, generated under Bismarck, for ministerial posts to be occupied by those who had the characteristics of officials rather than those of political leaders. There are two qualifications which need to be made here. First, while the parliamentary role in training ministers may have been sublimated by the administrative route, the minister is likely to have had executive and/or legislative experience through the territorial representative institutions (*conseils généraux, conseils municipaux*) and the office of mayor (see Becquart-Leclercq 1978). Secondly, the coming to power of the socialist government in 1981 appeared to reverse the tendency to recruit those with a civil service background to ministerial office which became especially strong under Giscard d'Estaing (see the translator's postscript in Birnbaum 1982). Whether this trend towards mandarin ascent will re-establish itself in subsequent governments remains an open question.

Perhaps the clearest tie between a ministerial career and parliament is found in Britain where most Cabinet members are also members of the House of Commons. The continuity between a parliamentary career and a ministerial career is strengthened by a range of junior ministerial posts (Secretaries of State or Ministers of State below the rank of Cabinet Minister and Parliamentary Private Secretaries). If one excludes newly elected MPs, very young and very old MPs, and those ineligible on personal grounds, such as poor physical or mental health, then there is a 'compulsion to draft half the eligible MPs into government' (Rose 1974: 363). Progress through the posts usually follows patterns of performance, seniority and experience in lower tasks, as well as standing with the party and the Prime Minister (see Headey 1974). Within this system it is possible to conceive of the House of Commons as a 'school for ministers'. However, it is not a school which gives the parliamentarian a particularly good training in the workings of the executive. Junior ministerial posts vary in the range of activities they cover, yet Headey (1974: 286) notes that junior ministers are 'all too often given miscellaneous dogsbody duties which leave them cut-off from the mainstream of policy-making and politicking'. This argument is endorsed by Rose (1974: 365) who suggests that

the existence of an established hierarchy of titles among the ranks of ministers provides a clear progression of jobs within the executive. It makes possible and probable for Cabinet ministers to undergo extensive role socialisation for years prior to reaching Cabinet. . . . But the job of a junior minister was not designed as a training ground for Cabinet ministers. The fact that service in such a post is virtually a *sine qua non* for Cabinet office does not assure that the time spent in these qualifying posts necessarily imparts skills used in higher offices.

Despite the progression between MP, junior ministerial position and Cabinet office, it can scarcely be argued in Britain that parliament offers a training ground for political leaders of the sort discussed by Weber for the simple reason that parliamentary activity, and even junior ministerial office, does not bring the aspiring Cabinet member into routine contact with the world of executive policy-making.

In Germany it is tempting to reach a similar conclusion.

The office of *parlamentarischer Staatssekretär* was introduced in 1967 based upon the British model of a gradation of ministerial offices (Rausch 1976). Like Britain, the role of *parlamentarischer Staatssekretär* varies from ministry to ministry, and minister to minister. Yet despite some differences, such as the power of the *parlamentarischer Staatssekretär* to stand in for a minister in Cabinet meetings, and the tendency to recruit parliamentarians with an established specialism as *parlamentarische Staatssekretäre* for posts related to their specialist knowledge, a similar conclusion about the position of *parlamentarischer Staatssekretär* to the position of junior ministers in Britain can be reached. They fulfil a variety of functions for ministers, frequently dealing with parliament and party, yet they are not routinely involved in the processes of policy-making within the executive organisations (Rausch 1976: 227).

However, there is a substantial difference between the role of parliament in ministerial recruitment in Britain and Germany. In Germany, parliament is only one arena among many for schooling politicians, not only in the art of political debate and persuasion, but also in the realities of leading governmental organisations (see Kaltefleiter 1976). German ministerial recruitment involves recruiting from a variety of backgrounds and experiences including from among those who were once party officials, prominent members of the *Bundestag* committees, members of a *Land* government, or those with a background in the civil service. Access to ministerial office usually requires experience of a leadership position in more than one of these areas:

The criteria for identifying those who are of Cabinet material appear to be almost invariably that the aspiring Cabinet member has proved him or herself in other positions of leadership. A purely civil service career alone is unlikely to open the door in a ministerial career, neither is a career within the party organisation alone. (Kaack 1971: 671)

In Germany, a political career is more likely to offer the minister experience of the operation of government, whether it is as an activist in *Bundestag* permanent committees or as a member of a *Land* government. Because of this it is possible to suggest that parliament in Germany is part of a wider training for political leadership of the form outlined by Weber. This pattern does not exist to the same extent in France or Britain despite the apparent similarity between the post of junior minister and *parlamentarischer Staatssekretär*.

CONCLUSION

In the first three of the four important dimensions of the role of parliament in a bureaucracy, the degree to which parliament has a negative role in approving legislation, approving the budget and the degree to which it subjects the executive to scrutiny, the European and American experiences contrast strongly with each other. While there are significant differences within Europe, above all the more developed collaboration between executive departments and permanent committees in Germany, in Europe the legislature is largely dominated by the executive. Legislatures in France, Germany and Britain do not initiate legislation to any significant degree, they are peripherally involved in the budgetary process and party cohesion and institutional limitations serve to restrict the scope of powerful scrutiny of executive actions by the legislatures. In contrast, the influence of Congress is pervasive in each of these three areas.

In the selection of political leaders the US Congress potentially offers more scope for bringing would-be members of the executive into contact with the daily world of executive policy-making (Rose 1974: 364–5), yet despite the fact that a few top appointees have had congressional experience, Congress does not provide a pool of recruits from which the President can routinely fill senior executive posts. In France, the role of parliament is important in legitimating aspiring ministers, even those who make their way to office via the 'mandarin ascent' route, yet it cannot be classed as a training ground for politicians who have to mobilise public support for their own political goals (see also

Chapter 7). In Britain, the shortcomings of the parliamentary career for training politicians lies in the unlikelihood that such a career will provide even one skilled in mobilising support with close contact with executive policy-making. In Germany, parliament is one among many institutions in which Cabinet members are likely to have worked, which together increase the chance of acquiring both forms of political skills.

5 Interest Groups and Bureaucracy

When W.C. Fields wanted to introduce a juggling routine into his portrayal of Micawber in the film of *David Copperfield*, his reply to the suggestion that this was inappropriate because Dickens had not included one in his book was that Dickens would have done if he had thought of it. In interpreting Weber for this comparative analysis it is tempting to argue the same for the role of interest groups in a bureaucratic system of government. That their role is important is stressed by the fact that, excluding their interactions with other civil servants, senior civil servants interact with interest groups more frequently than with all other bodies and individuals, ministers included (Aberbach, Putnam and Rockman 1981: 215). Yet Weber gives interest groups relatively little prominence. The question of why Weber devotes so little space to them is not one that can be approached in this study. Weber was certainly aware of their influence. For example, he discussed group influence as an important component of political representation (Weber 1972: 174–6) and saw them as a crucial force in understanding the growth of government since many of the state's new tasks were partly 'foisted on it by interests' (Weber 1972: 561).

Weber appears to be rather ambivalent about the effects of interest group activity in a bureaucratic form of government. On the one hand groups had the potential of cultivating the form of political leadership which was so necessary to prevent a bureaucratic system from degenerating into rule by officials; along with party organisation, local politics and journalism, interest-group activity offered one extra-parliamentary arena for the conduct of political action and training politicians in the skills of mobilising support and of compomise (Weber 1958: 533). On the other hand Weber pointed to the dangers in including groups in the process of policy-making in the case of the integration of business interests into the German machinery for economic management during the first world war. He opposed the extension of this machinery into the peacetime governmental system since it was 'fantasy' to expect that 'it would be the state which would be the regulator of the economy. The reverse would be the case. The bankers and capitalist entrepreneurs would then be the unlimited and unconstrained masters of the state' (Weber 1958: 255).

How, then, can one fit interest groups into a study of bureaucracy while retaining a Weberian perspective? The answer put forward here is that the *influence* of interest groups, which Weber (1972: 123) clearly separated from the exercise of formal legitimate *authority*, serves to limit the exercise of political leadership over the administrative apparatus. The reasons for arguing this are similar to those outlined in Chapter 3 in the discussion of the implications of conflicts and divisions within the administrative apparatus. In its purest form, bureaucracy is a monocratic system. There is a concentration within a single figure or institution of the ability to give direction to hierarchical inferiors. Where a system of rule involves the inclusion of 'compromises between colliding interests', the scope for the independence of lower levels for the higher levels within the administration becomes greater (Weber 1972: 123). Thus, even though a purely monocratic system is not found in either France, Germany, Britain or the United States, by reference to the ideal type one can recognise that it becomes difficult for a political leader—or anyone else for that matter—to give direction to the administrative organisation formally under its command when what the organisation does results from its interactions with the groups with which it comes into contact rather than from direction from above. This point is made explicit when Weber writes of

This development which seeks to place the concrete technical knowledge of the interests in the service of the professionally-educated official certainly has a significant future and increases the power of the bureaucracy still further. . . . The role that interest groups are likely in future to play inside the administrative apparatus cannot be discussed here. (1972: 576)

This is similar to the argument put forward by Beer when he discusses the 'professional bureaucratic' complexes in Washington which consist of a

core of officials with scientific and professional training. The bureaucratic core also normally works in close cooperation with two other components: certain interested legislators, especially the chairmen of relevant specialised sub-committees, and the spokesmen for the group that benefits from the program initially brought into existence by bureaucrats and politicians. (Beer 1977: 9–10)

This suggests that members of a bureaucracy may develop common values and interests with those within the same policy sector, whether they are bureaucrats, legislators or members of interest groups, rather than with their hierarchical superiors. This has consequences for political leadership similar to those set out in this interpretation of Weber: 'However cooperative these professions may be with their fellows in the same discipline and program, their dispersion among the many vertical hierarchies leaves them little opportunity or incentive for concerted action toward common national priorities and problems' (Beer 1978: 22).

Interest groups are important in the influence they exert on the policy process in each of the four countries in this study, and they influence the actions of officials at a variety of levels within the administration. Weber himself hinted that relatively few factory inspectors could resist the temptation to 'bend at the first puff of air blown at them by commercial interests' (1958: 263). So should we not end this chapter here with a statement about the ubiquity of the pluralist constraints that operate upon a government through pressure-group influence and a few references to interesting case studies in each of the four countries? Fortunately, there is a little more that can be said about the role of interest groups, since it is possible to make broad characterisations about the way in which interest groups are involved in the policy-making process in different countries, despite the variability of influence, modes of operation and aims of different interest groups within a single nation (see Richardson 1982).

While there are a variety of ways in which the patterns of interest-group activity can be evaluated, the variable to be explored in this chapter is the scope for those who are at the head of government departments within a bureaucratic system—whether political leaders or officials—to use the authority of the state to pursue their own policy goals. Conversely, it explores the degree to which the exercise of state authority is largely contingent upon the outcome of group bargaining. The crucial concept here is the notion of 'non-negotiable' policy (see Page 1982; Richardson 1982), since to be able to make policy non-negotiable allows the senior members of the executive to pursue their objectives. This ability to make issues or the exercise of the powers of the state non-negotiable is one of the defining features of public authority (cf. Weber 1972: 822), and leads us to ask the following question of each of the four countries: how far is the *authority* of the bureaucratic state capable of being exercised despite the ubiquity of interest-group influence through the ability in a bureaucratic system of government to make issues non-negotiable?

ISSUE NETWORKS IN THE UNITED STATES

The American experience offers perhaps the clearest example of the weakness of public authority in the face of interest-group pressures where the scope for non-negotiable policy initiatives is narrow. (For a general discussion, see Lowi 1969; Wolin 1981.) The argument that policy-making in Washington is negotiated between a variety of communities composed of interest-group representatives, officials from government agencies and members of congressional committees and sub-committees has been consistently put forward since at least the 1930s (see Freeman 1955). The imagery used to describe the relationship between interest groups, congressional committees and government agencies is often that of the 'iron triangles', with different agencies, congressional committees and sub-committees, and constellations of interest groups forming a series of relatively stable communities which are the focus for policy-making in Washington (see Clark 1981). The image suggests that the three sets of institutions define a set of powerful forces in Washington which are virtually impervious to any attempt by those outside to influence the development of policy within the policy areas covered by the iron triangles. Cater's (1964) study of the 'sub-government of defense', for example, shows how policy-making for defence was dominated by the Pentagon, the armed services and Defense Appropriations Committees in Congress and interests such as the Aerospace Industries Association and the General Dynamics Corporation. Other areas which have been cited as the focus for sub-government by the iron triangles include the fields of social security, health, the Veterans' Administration, and the Army Corps of Engineers (see Heclo 1978: 105; *National Journal*, 28 March 1981).

Heclo (1978; see also Seidman 1980; Kaufman 1981a) argues that the iron triangle image presents a picture of stability of relationships between groups, the legislature and executive within Washington that is misleading; the relationships have become far more fluid and complex. In the 1970s there was a rapid expansion of the number of groups and their representatives in Washington. Estimates vary on the precise dimensions of the expansion, but all observers agree that the expansion has been rapid and large. Walker (1983: 394) gives an estimated growth in the total number of lobby groups active in Washington from around 500 in the 1920s to 1700 in 1980, although in some particular policy areas the growth has been even more striking than that, with the number of groups involved in policy-making for American Indian Affairs growing from sixteen groups at the time of Freeman's (1965) study in 1960 to at least forty-eight in 1980. Although interest-group representation is nothing new in Washington, the huge expansion in the 1970s is only 'a mere outgrowth of old tendencies . . . in the same sense that a 16-lane spaghetti interchange is the mere elaboration of a county crossroads' (Heclo 1978: 97). Colella and Beam (1981) argue similarly that interest groups have grown up on the principle 'for every Macdonalds there is a Burger King'; groups are set up to counter the influence of other groups. In addition, as the US Advisory Commission on Inter-governmental Relations (1981b: 15) noted, there is a tendency for government programmes themselves to gener-ate interest groups by creating a 'policy niche' which can be occupied by a new group. Thus, for example, the National Environmental Policy Act 1969 gave birth to the Natural Resources Defense Council.

There are two characteristics of many of the new groups. First, the groups are heavily Washington-oriented with few having significant membership or national organisations (US Advisory Commission on Intergovernmental Relations 1981a: 202). Second, these groups have become so closely integrated into the policy-making system in Washington that they are routinely classed as 'inside players' in the policy process along with the judiciary, the President, Congress and the executive agencies (US Advisory Commission on Intergovernmental Relations 1981b).

These groups have transformed the process of policy-making from rather stable networks of autonomous groups composed of members of the legislature, the executive and groups associated with the iron triangle imagery, to a complex of 'issue networks' consisting of 'a large number of participants with quite variable degrees of mutual commit-ment . . . participants move in and out of the networks constantly. Rather than groups united in dominance over a program, no one, so far as one can tell, is in control of the policies and issues' (Heclo 1978: 102). The networks tend to specialise in relatively narrow areas of policy and develop highly specialised technical knowledge which makes parti-cipation difficult for those who are unfamiliar with the issues concerning the network.

These fluid networks are important because they affect the appointment of personnel to key executive positions (see Chapter 2). Moreover, the interest groups affect in a more routine way the development of policy within executive agencies. Kaufman's (1981a: 71) study offers direct evidence of the role of groups in the everyday working of a bureau. Agency chiefs in his study 'strove—or were forced—to maintain relations' with a variety of groups. Some of these were 'natural backers' of the agency; those upon whom the agency could normally rely to support it publicly as well as in Congress. In addition it also sought to maintain close relations with those groups hostile to the agency even when such a relationship was 'foisted' upon the agency by the persistence of the group. The agencies devoted much effort to maintaining these contacts with the groups.

Unanimous denunciation, even for mutually contradictory reasons, is assumed to result in decreased support in Congress, reduced cooperation in the executive branch and diminished compliance with bureau policies in the outside world. Unanimous approbation, on the other hand, is regarded as too much to expect in an arena of diverse, often clashing, interests.

In order to mobilise support, from some quarters at least, the bureaus in Kaufman's study sought to explain and sell their policies to interest groups. This frequently was aimed at securing that 'avoidable irritants and provocations contained in agency proposals could be eliminated or softened' (Kaufman 1981a: 66).

The notion that the agencies themselves pursue strategies to seek to manage their relations with groups, and themselves to a degree manipulate interest groups (see also Seidman 1980: 169) offers a valuable counter to a view that executive agencies are merely the passive victims of group pressures. However, in the United States system, groups constitute a strong constraint upon executive policy-making which, along with other features of the American system of government, such as the structure of the executive itself and the structure and influence of Congress, serve to fragment executive authority and limit the scope for non-negotiable policy-making.

PRESSURED-GROUP POLITICS IN FRANCE

The integration of interest groups into the policy-making process as negotiators with legislative and executive groups in the United States contrasts strongly with the role of interest groups in France where the 'traditional suspicion of any encroachment of private interests on public policy' (Hayward 1983: 62) suggests a weaker role for groups in the policy-making process. More specifically, for the purposes of this study, this tradition suggests two important features of the relationship between the executive and interest groups in France. First, it suggests that the state is in control of the relationship that it has with interest groups. Unlike the position in the United States, the French tradition gives primacy to the state deciding which groups it listens to and, consequently, how it acts upon what it hears (Suleiman 1974: 337). As Hayward (1983: 62) suggests, the French tradition of consultation inclines 'some civil servants to regard consultation as the historic duty of vassals to advise their feudal lord'. Secondly, and following on from this, civil servants see a clear division, if not outright contradiction, between the 'public interest' which the civil service sees itself as serving, and the 'special pleading' of self-interested groups (see also Dyson 1980).

Suleiman's (1974) interviews with senior officials in France serve to reinforce this picture of state–interest group relations. French top officials, like their counterparts in the other three nations in this study, stated that they had fairly frequent contacts with groups: 70 per cent of *directeurs* had meetings with groups either 'very often' or 'almost every day'. However, they were reluctant to answer questions about how they were influenced by groups, since the notion that one can be swayed by interests was linked in their minds with weakness, and possibly even with corruption. Suleiman (1974: 329) summarises the position thus.

Interest or pressure groups exist to defend and champion their interests by means of pressure on the administration. The administration, on the other hand, must resist pressure coming from those who seek particularistic aims. Just as the administration manifests a scarcely disguised antipathy towards the deputy because of his ability to embroil it in 'politics' and his tireless devotion to the petty problems of his constituents, so it sees interest groups as also attempting to embroil the administration in conflicts that revolve around particularistic demands

From the perspective of the legitimacy of the exercise as well as the sheer time it would appear to take up, civil servants in France believe that they should avoid pressure-group demands upon their attention.

Suleiman's analysis takes us somewhat beyond the formal denial by top officials of group influence by showing that civil servants distinguish between 'illegitimate' (termed 'pressure' groups, a rather derogatory label among the top officials in Suleiman's study) and 'legitimate' groups (termed 'professional bodies'). Such legitimate groups included above all the larger industrial firms which enjoyed close relationships with the different branches (*directions*) of the Ministry of Industrial Development. In the *directions* concerning sectors of industry which were dominated by large firms, such as fuel, petroleum and chemicals, there was 'little hope for firms not included in the network' of relations surrounding the particular *direction* 'to receive equal treatment' (Suleiman 1974: 344).

Nevertheless, even though there is scope for the inclusion of groups within the close network of contacts of civil servants, this does not make them the 'insiders' in the policy-making process that they appear to be in the United States since the relationship with the state is clearly an uneven one. The state reserves for itself the right to make non-negotiable decisions even in areas covered by groups generally acknowledged to be among the most powerful. This is shown clearly in the case of the *Fédération Nationale des Syndicats d'Exploitants Agricoles* (FNSEA), the most influential of the French farmers' unions, which has a relationship with the state which is argued to approximate a 'corporatist' relationship (Keeler 1981). Doubtless, the involvement between the FNSEA and the Ministry of Agriculture is a very close one, and doubtless the FNSEA is given a variety of privileges by the state denied other farmers' groups. However, Keeler's own evidence shows the dominance of the state in this relationship and the clear scope for unilateral, non-negotiable decisions on the part of the state. The state chose to ignore the FNSEA and collaborated with its youth wing, the *Centre National des Jeunes Agriculteurs* (CNJA), at the time of the important agricultural modernisation policies of the 1960s, and the state encouraged the takeover of the FNSEA, dominated in the 1960s by an older generation which regarded 'statist bureaucrats' as their permanent enemy, by the younger members of the CNJA who were far more sympathetic to the government's approach to agricultural modernisation. Furthermore, the leadership of the FNSEA is consistently accused by its members of having sold out to the government.

This suggests a model fundamentally different from the American where the scope of governmental action which can evade the claims of groups is relatively narrow. Certainly, many policies in France involve the participation of interest groups, and are subject to the pluralistic pressures of group activity. However, in France it is possible for the government to derive policies and priorities without their involvement and sell these policies to the groups afterwards. As Hayward (1983: 68) suggests, in France 'the executive is so powerful that the peak organisations are more like pressured groups than pressure groups.'

RULE BY INTEREST GROUPS IN GERMANY?

In 1955 Theodor Eschenburg's *Herrschaft der Verbände?* (*Dominance by Groups?*) argued that the under-assertive state (*Unterstaat*) towards which West Germany appeared to be developing was the initial reaction to the over-assertive state (*Überstaat*) of the National Socialist era; the Germans had developed an under-respect for the principle of state authority (a *Staatsunlust*), and an over-respect for pluralism, and in particular for interest groups. In Eschenburg's formulation, groups looked set to predominate in the German policy-making process; ministries were staffed with interest-group representatives, as were the specialist *Bundestag* committees. Even in the field of the permanent civil service, groups were sustaining their claims to influencing personnel policy. Eschenburg cites the case of a permanent *Staatssekretär* in Lower Saxony, Bojunga, who was dismissed in favour of a Catholic because he was associated with a set of school reforms opposed by Catholics even though, as Eschenburg suggests, he was little more than a ministerial aide and adviser in this case. This offered one of many clear contradictions to Eschenburg between group involvement and the public authority of the government and its administrative staff. It showed that 'whoever dares to act against the group risks losing his position. Thus through political means the duty of civil servants to obey is eroded and replaced by dependence on the group' (Eschenburg 1963: 25).

While Eschenburg's argument was heavily criticised (for a discussion of the criticisms see Rausch 1976), the basic thesis, that dependence upon group pluralism limited the scope for the exercise of public authority, that the scope for the government pursuing non-negotiable policies is extremely limited where groups become insiders in the policy-making process is one that appears to be upheld by subsequent studies. Braunthal's (1965: 231) study of the *Bundesverband Deutscher Industriegesellschaften* argues that Eschenburg's thesis has a 'good deal of validity', although he points out that the 'party chieftains [in the Christian Democratic Union] must balance conflicting demands, and must work out compromises and concessions in order to keep business, labour, agricultural and other forces well enough satisfied to stay within the party' (Braunthal 1965: 348).

Undoubtedly, since Eschenburg wrote his book the influence exerted by interest groups on personnel within ministries has declined as the parties became more important (see Dyson 1977), although the two are not necessarily mutually exclusive (see also, von Beyme 1983). Eschenburg's thesis draws heavily, but not exclusively, on the influence of groups in the appointment of governmental personnel and, as von Beyme (1983: 53) points out:

In a country where very few new Cabinets and even reshuffles occur less frequently than in the American presidential or the British parliamentary system, interest groups cannot concentrate exclusively on launching their people into the power centres. Their main efforts are concentrated on the everyday decision-making process.

That the central thrust of the thesis is still a valid one, however, is suggested by the works of Ellwein and Dyson. Ellwein's (1974: 486) survey of interest-group activity in West Germany concludes that the group system has a 'conservative effect and creates limits on the room for manoeuvre in policy-making which can make the social system incapable of innovation.' Ellwein cites as an example of this the opposition of industrial groups which, in the absence of any countervailing pressures, managed to obstruct the development of environmental protection policies. Dyson (1982b) argues that in Germany there are styles characterised by a more assertive role for the state *vis à vis* interest groups ('activism' and 'regulation'), and more passive styles ('concertation' and 'status preservation') in which the state's actions or inaction results from group responses to its initiatives. The case studies he cites show the limitations of the more assertive styles and the importance of accommodating group interests; delays and shifts in nuclear policy reflected the emergence of environmental groups; reforms of health policy were 'characterised by a stalemate of opposed interests and consequent immobility of policy'; and in economic policy the state relied heavily on 'the social partners [i.e. capital and labour groups] to work out acceptable economic solutions'. To this one could add Reissert's (1980: 175) discussion of the 'immobility' in the system of grants for local government due in part to the 'antagonistic interests of local government lobbyists'. The requirement that the state devises policies which are designed to avoid conflict within the political system is further reinforced by the divisions within state institutions themselves (see Scharpf, Reissert and Schnabel 1976; Dyson 1982b). The resulting 'collaborative style' or policy-making which 'emphasises the need to accommodate group press-

ures in order to maintain social peace' suggests a far more
limited role for a non-negotiable sphere of state activity than
Britain (see below) and certainly France.

INTEREST-GROUP CONSULTATION IN BRITAIN

On the basis of much of the 'ungovernability' literature in
Britain (see King 1975; Beer 1982) one might expect to find
a similar set of pluralistic constraints upon executive
policy-making in Britain to those found in Germany and
perhaps even the United States, in which the scope of
non-negotiable policy-making within the executive is highly
limited. Thus Beer, for example, talks of a 'pluralist
stagnation' in Britain produced by the 'new group politics'.
The expansion of the state has generated an increased
vulnerability of government to group pressures.

In a free country, the enormous new powers that government
exercises over producer and consumer groups at the same time
puts these groups in a position to frustrate those powers by
refusing their consent. (Beer 1982: 14)

The evidence to suggest that government is conducted
routinely by the executive on the basis of group consultation
is extremely well documented in Richardson and Jordan's
Governing Under Pressure (1979), according to which even
the government departments themselves could be regarded
in the same light as the interest groups as competitors and
negotiators in the complex and interdependent world of
executive policy-making.

Undoubtedly, the evidence is strong to suggest that the
British style of policy-making (cf. Richardson 1982), like the
German, lays stress on group participation and the avoidance of 'electoral politics and public conflict in order to
reach consensus or "accommodation" in the labyrinth of
consultative machinery which has developed' (Jordan and
Richardson 1982: 81). However, as Jordan and Richardson
stress, a policy style refers to 'standard operating procedures' and '*preferred* operating procedures'. This suggests

the possibility that preferred procedures are those which can, under certain circumstances, be abandoned when the desire to achieve a policy outcome is stronger than the preference for the standard procedures. In short, it suggests the possibility that government may retain a consultative style while still possessing the capacity to retain key issues as non-negotiable.

Certainly the rhetoric of the Conservative Party, with its anti-corporatist strategy (see Jordan and Richardson 1982), referring to an explicit intention to pursue policies unpopular with apparently powerful interest groups, suggests that the scope of non-negotiable policy-making is relatively wide. Yet despite Jordan and Richardson's suggestions to the contrary, there appears to be some substance behind the rhetoric. In the case of one set of groups who were, in the 1970s, conventionally assumed to have privileged access to policy negotiation within the executive, the local authority associations (see Rhodes 1981), one can see that beginning with the onset of financial stringency and the consequent cuts in local government grants after 1976, the contact between the associations in the key area of finance looked far more like central government announcing its decision to the assembled representatives of local authorities than a real negotiation in which substantial modifications were made to central policies on the basis of the representations of the associations. In addition, throughout the period of the 1979 Conservative government, a number of key issues, such as the structure of the grant system, the sale of council houses and the abolition of supplementary rates, have been added to the issue of grant levels as policy areas which are non-negotiable with local authority associations. The apparent bargaining with local associations that persisted until the 1970s was ended with the onset of financial stringency; this is confirmed by the apparently deliberate rejections of the consultative machinery, such as when the minister responsible for local government announced to the press the outcome of a meeting with the associations before it had taken place. The government has also displayed a similar preparedness to ignore the expressed interests of other groups such as trade unions, the Confederation of British

Industry and the Police Federation in key areas of government policy.

Of course, one must not exaggerate the extent of the rejection of interest-group consultation and negotiation. In most policy areas consultation persists. For example local authorities are consulted on a variety of matters outside the key issue of finance, and there is evidence to suggest that this consultation influences government policy (Dunleavy and Rhodes 1983), and business and labour groups are important in the functioning of the Manpower Services Commission (see Jordan and Richardson 1982). However, the experiences of the Conservative government since 1979 have underlined a feature of consultation underlined by Jordan (1981: 107) 'consultation is about exclusion', referring to the fact that inevitably some groups are excluded from the policy-making process, while others are included. British government appears to have greater discretion in defining not only which groups are included and excluded, but in defining issues which exclude any substantial group involvement or negotiation. Certainly this conclusion is supported in the contrast between Britain and the United States—Jordan (1981: 121) refers to the less marked development of 'issue networks' in Britain compared with the United States. It is also supported by the contrast with West Germany—Dyson (1982b: 45) argues that 'the idea of a sphere of non-negotiable policy has, therefore, been less apparent [in Germany] than in Britain.' It would be mistaken to equate the role of interest groups as fragmenting executive authority in the United States and even Germany with the *convention* of consultation found in Britain.

CONCLUSION

Outwardly, the role of pressure groups and their relationship with the executive in each of the four countries are very similar. They are ubiquitously consulted on a number of policy issues. In addition, the more closely one pays attention to the actual implementation of policy, the more ubiquitous and pervasive the influence of group pressures appears (see Hayward 1982). Furthermore, one could argue that if one were to take top executives' anticipations of group reactions into account, the role of groups in policy-making would appear even greater.

However, in this chapter distinctions have been drawn about the way in which interest groups constrain policy-making in each of the four countries. More specifically, the distinction has been drawn between the United States and Germany on the one hand, and France and Britain on the other. The distinction is one of degree of group involvement and the scope of non-negotiable policy-making, with non-negotiable policy more likely to be found in Britain and France than in Germany and the United States. The implications of this are that in Germany and the United States executive leadership, whether by officials or politicians, is substantially constrained by the constellation of outside pressures. Here the systems are unlikely to be a system of *Beamtenherrschaft* because the administrative system is relatively open to interest-group pressures. In Britain and France, on the other hand, the potential for either political leadership or *Beamtenherrschaft* is greater since the executive has greater discretion over which interest groups it negotiates with and, probably more importantly, when.

6 Collegiality, Advice and Courts

This chapter discusses three further limitations to the development of the dominance of officials in a bureaucratic system of government which can be found in Weber's writings. *Collegiality* refers to the principle of sharing authority within the framework of a particular system of rule. As Albrow (1970: 47) explains, 'bureaucracy [for Weber] meant that, at each stage of the official hierarchy, one person, and one person only, had the responsibility for taking a decision. As soon as others were involved in taking that decision, *as of right*, then the collegial system was being employed.' Weber (1972: 158–67) discusses a number of forms of collegiality in his section on the forms of limitation upon ideal types of authority. The most important for our purposes is the form of collegiality found in European Cabinet systems which can be found when

there is a formally monocratic *primus inter pares*, but directives are only issued after discussion with other formally equal members and deviation from the views of the *collegium* means a destruction of the *collegium* by resignations and thus endangers the position of the monocratic leader. (Weber 1972: 159)

Weber discusses this as one of the means through which any of his ideal types of rule can be limited, not specifically as a limitation to the exercise of rational-legal rule or of the resulting potential for *Beamtenherrschaft*. However, in the case of rational-legal government, collegiality detracts from the hierarchical structure of bureaucratic government and causes delays as well as limitations on the formal authority of the monocratic government, whether exercised by a politician or an official. However, it is also possible to link this with a limitation on the development of *Beamtenherrschaft*. Not only does this form of collegiality permit the monocratic leader to surround himself with experts and thus counter the 'rule through knowledge' of the officials in the administrative staff (see below), the existence of collegiality is one means of countering the trend towards satrapic conflicts between different branches of the administration which lead to the increased power of the official (discussed in Chapter 3). The collegial principle, especially in the form of the Cabinet principle, permits an expression, and political means of resolution, of conflicts which might otherwise degenerate into courtly intrigues within the top of the executive branch.

It is certainly desirable that the current process of taking politically important decisions, which leads to satrapic conflicts of different bureaus with one another be replaced by a system of collegial dialogue of important questions between the *Reichschancellor* and all Secretaries of State. (Weber 1958: 423–4)

Following on from this, and also examined under the heading of collegiality, is the ability of the monocratic leader of a bureaucratic form of government to seek advice through some form of personal staff. As discussed in Chapter 2, the power of officials derives primarily from their specialised knowledge. The political leader is a dilettante compared with the specialist, and can maintain superiority over the specialists through employing the advice of specialists:

This form of collegial authority is thus the typical form in which the ruler, who increasingly becomes a 'dilettante' evaluates technical information and, although this point is often ignored, seeks to use this form of advice to defend himself against the growing preeminance of technical knowledge and maintain his own dominant position. (Weber 1972: 574)

The second section of this chapter examines the degree to which ministers use their own personal staffs in the development of policy in the ministry (for a discussion of presidential and prime ministerial staffs, see Cohen 1980; Mayntz 1980a; Rose 1980a; Salaman 1981; Andrews 1983; Weller 1983).

The role of courts as a limitation upon the development of dominance by officials stems from the nature of bureaucratic government itself as a form of rational-legal authority (Weber 1972: 158). Governments can be 'bound by legal norms and by acquired subjective rights'. Since government activities and competences are legally defined, ultimately largely through constitutional norms, government activities can be initiated and prevented through legal means. The courts, of course, deal with a variety of issues involving government institutions, from the case of a man assaulted by a post office employee, to handing over the Watergate tapes. The third section of this chapter will look at the role of courts in a particularly important role in their relationship with the executive; that of the courts' *judicial review* of the activities undertaken in the name of government.

CABINETS AND COLLEGIAL DECISION-MAKING

It is important to distinguish between decisions taken *involving* secretaries and ministers and decisions taken *collectively* by Cabinets. Mackie and Hogwood (1983) identify seven ways in which decision-making by Cabinet members may take place. First, there are *unilateral* decisions taken by the minister as head of his department; second, there are decisions taken as a result of *internalised coordination* through which a minister himself decides to take the initiative in negotiating decisions with other department; third, there are *bilateral decisions* resulting from discussions between a minister and another department; fourth, there are *multilateral decisions* which result from more or less informal discussions between several ministers; fifth, there are *Cabinet committee* decisions in which decisions are effectively taken by a formally constituted sub-group of the Cabinet; sixth, there are *Cabinet* decisions in which the full Cabinet takes an effective decision; and seventh, there are *party decisions* which result from a process of inter- or intra-party discussions in which ministers are involved *qua* leading members of their party.

The evidence suggests that collegial decision-making, in the form of Hogwood and Mackie's sixth variety of decision-making type, is relatively rare in each of the four countries. Studies of the United States have traditionally pointed to the weakness of Cabinet government. The composition of the Cabinet varies from administration to administration. Normally it contains the Secretaries of the executive departments, but occasionally others (see Seidman 1980: 246–7), such as the Director of the Office of Management and the Budget (OMB), presidential assistants and the Speaker of the House of Representatives. Other aspects of its functioning, such as its meeting cycle and the formality of its organisation, also vary from administration to administration. As a collective decision-making body its weakness is less variable. Fenno's (1959) classic study indicates the 'essential powerlessness' of the Cabinet in the United States; it is weak in giving policy advice; communication between agencies usually only occurs 'on the lucky chance that something might pop up during casual Cabinet conversations'; the Cabinet is unable to settle inter-agency disagreement, with Cabinet resolutions either ignored or subject to highly different interpretations. Its development as a collective decision-making body is limited by the 'basic pluralism of the American political system', not least through the statutory basis of the authority of the Cabinet Secretary which largely removes the possibility of the President using some form of hierarchical authority over Cabinet members, short of replacement, as a means of encouraging collective decision-making. It is for this reason that Cabinet weakness should not be associated with presidential strength; after his examination of the role of the Cabinet and the various groups and networks involving Cabinet members, Helmer (1981: 53) argues that 'in the organizational complex for which the short appellation is the Cabinet, there is nothing so simple as presidential leadership.'

That the US experience of Cabinet government diverges from the European experience was discussed by

Weber: European nations adopted what Weber regarded as the British model of the Cabinet system, while the US did not. Certainly the traditional view of the British Cabinet sees the Cabinet as a collective decision-making body with supreme power and authority within policy-making in Britain. As one textbook (Hanson and Walles 1975: 97) has it: 'most legislative as well as administrative initiative comes from the Cabinet which derives its authority from the electoral decision that has given its supporters a majority in the House of Commons.' Not only is the Cabinet important in influencing policy-making, it exercises this influence as a *collectivity*. Its collective nature is, according to a traditional view, strengthened by the doctrine of 'collective responsibility', according to which responsibility for a Cabinet decision is shared among all the members of the Cabinet, with a minister resigning should he not be prepared to take this responsibility. There is the further fact that members of the Cabinet are drawn from the same political party and thus share common political outlooks and aspirations for their party's success, as well as the fact that the Cabinet is dependent upon majority support in parliament and is likely to seek agreement across the range of opinion within the government's parliamentary party through compromise between the representatives of different strands of opinion usually included in the Cabinet. One of the major questions asked about the institution of the Cabinet is whether the Prime Minister is *primus inter pares* or actually dominates the Cabinet: either way, the Cabinet is argued, according to a more traditional view, to be the focal point of the policy-making process in Britain.

Undoubtedly, this picture of the influence of the Cabinet as well as its collective identity is a misleading one. While the Cabinet in Britain undoubtedly serves as a strong focus for political authority (Rose 1980b) in a way that the US Cabinet does not, it is misleading to present the process of policy-making as one in which the Cabinet is, in the words of the 1918 Haldane committee, the 'mainspring of policy'. Richardson and Jordan (1979) show through a variety of case studies how 'very much in British politics can be understood without reference to the Cabinet'. The Cabinet does not routinely initiate policies; instead there are other forums of policy initiation, notably the network of relationships between interest groups and government departments. Neither do many decisions have to be referred to Cabinet. Tony Crosland, Education Secretary in the Labour government from 1965 to 1967 took very few matters of education policy to Cabinet (see Kogan, Crosland and Boyle 1971). Furthermore, its collective nature can be called into question. Edmund Dell (1980: 31), a former Labour Cabinet minister, stated that collective responsibility had little effective meaning, and that the 'public spectacle of the Cabinet in travail was a farce'. Richardson and Jordan (1979: 26) include in their evidence pointing to the limitations of the Cabinet as a collective decision-making body Barbara Castle's view that her expectation of Cabinet as colleagues discussing priorities was at variance with the actual practice of being 'surrounded by departmental enemies'. They conclude that 'at Cabinet level, those ministers with departmental responsibilities appear to view their pre-eminent task as the representation of that department (and often its associated clientèle)'. Furthermore, the collective identity is further reduced by the tendency of decisions to be taken in sub-groups of the Cabinet, Cabinet committees (Mackie and Hogwood 1983; for a view of their effect on cabinet government, see Crossman 1963).

Similarly, in Germany one can question whether the Cabinet principle provides a routine exercise of collegial leadership (see Mayntz 1980a). The Cabinet itself exists within a framework of interdepartmental committees, Cabinet committees and *ad hoc* relationships between ministers as one finds within the British Cabinet system (cf. Rausch 1976: 228–41). There exist some formal requirements that legislative proposals be approved by the Cabinet before being submitted to parliament, but these are usually subjected to the most cursory of discussions, if discussed at all. While the Federal Chancellor has *Richtlinienkompetenz* (ability to set guidelines for the individual ministers), Hennis (quoted in Rausch 1976: 186) states that 'ministers are not subordinates', their obligation to collegial government and the guidelines from the Chancellor are balanced by the

Ressortprinzip (the notion that the minister is constitutionally responsible for the actions of his department). While bounded by different constitutional traditions, the principle of a collegial authority having superiority over individual departments in which the Chancellor has powers of patronage and persuasion not possessed by his colleagues is similar to the British position. Also similar to Britain is the degree to which this model coexists with a 'sub-government' system in which decisions are taken without being referred to Cabinet, and where Cabinet decisions are frequently the legitimation of decisions taken elsewhere such as in Cabinet committees or interdepartmental committees (Mayntz 1980a: 155).

In France the dual nature of the executive, with a Prime Minister dependent upon support in the Assembly and the President of the Republic (since 1962) elected by popular majority complicates this picture of the European experience of a collegial body exercising supreme authority within the executive branch of government. The early years of the Fifth Republic perpetuated this duality in the form of a Cabinet Council (excluding the President) and the Council of Ministers (presided over by the President). With the expansion of presidential government, however, the

ambivalence was dissolved by the extinction of the parliamentarist Cabinet Council and the establishment of the Council of Ministers as a viable instrument of presidentialist governance. (Andrews 1981: 25)

The presidential Council of Ministers, however, has not functioned as a general collegial body which acts as the mainspring of government policy. Instead, meetings of the Council of Ministers have tended to become rather routine encounters legitimising decisions already taken outside the Council of Ministers and reporting actions taken within particular government departments; as Andrews (1981: 35) states, the meetings of the Council 'afforded scant opportunity for the working deliberations that resolve disagreements and settle problems'. Since the coming to power of President Mitterrand in 1981, Hayward (1983: 115–17) suggests, the

Council of Ministers has become less of a rubber stamp for decisions taken elsewhere, with greater encouragement of ministers to deliberate on policies outside their ministerial concerns. However, it is not possible at this stage to evaluate whether the Mitterrand presidency has brought about a fundamental and lasting transformation of the policy-making process in France in this respect.

In each of the four countries the role of the Cabinet falls far short of the collegial form of government discussed by Weber in so far as it suggests that a collective leadership should be responsible for decision-making. There are, of course, other forms of ministerial collaboration with other ministers in the form of institutions such as Cabinet committees (Hogwood and Mackie 1983) and interdepartmental committees (Mayntz and Scharpf 1975; de Baecque 1982), and in the United States a substantial portion of an agency head's time is taken up in affairs concerning relationships with other agencies and departments. The fact that in many policy areas, of which budgeting is the most important example, two or more ministries or agencies are interdependent and bargain and consult with each other does not however, constitute collegial leadership. None of these observations detracts from the general observation that policy-making in government rarely involves the collective deliberation of other ministers in the affairs of departments that are not their own.

Apart from policies to which political parties are publicly committed, decisions tend to be taken within differentiated sectors and networks and not by a collective 'government'. Mackie and Hogwood's (1983) comparative analysis shows that relatively few policy issues are referred to Cabinet, and that when they reach Cabinet they are not decided upon or even discussed in a manner which brings ministers to transcend their departmental interests and loyalties. Furthermore, the decisions taken do not even conform to the picture of Cabinet setting 'broad policy guidelines' as Mackie and Hogwood (1983: 31) show:

What goes to Cabinet tend to be individual issues and not consideration of policy areas. For example, Cabinet may be asked to take a decision about the closure of an individual industrial plant rather than to reappraise all aspects of regional policy. In dealing with politically important issues, Cabinet members inevitably have a fragmentary picture of the broader policy context in which the issues have arisen.

This tendency for decisions to be taken within the context of differentiated policy networks rather than through collegial institutions can be termed a 'sub-government' characterisation of policy-making (Rose 1980b; Jordan 1981). Of course, there are substantial differences between each of the four countries from the perspective of the ability of the President or Prime Minister to influence policy-making within these 'sub-governments' (Rose 1980b), with central institutions such as the presidential staff in France, the Federal Chancellor's Office in Germany and the Treasury in Britain reinforcing the influence of the President and Prime Minister in such a way that it is possible to speak of sub-government coexisting with government. In the United States, the fragmentation of political authority means that there is sub-government without government. However, this section has not been concerned with an analysis of the role of the President and Prime Minister. Rather, to affirm the importance of sub-government is to point to the weakness of the collegial principle as it operates in France, Germany, the United States and Britain as a limitation to the development of the power of the official.

ADVISERS AND MINISTERS' PERSONAL STAFFS

Few elected leaders of the executive are short of advice, if one understands this to mean the receipt of views about what is desirable or prudent. Advice can come from statutory or non-statutory advisory or consultative bodies, legislative committees, specialist commissions (committees within a political party, for example), in addition to the advice that emanates from pressure groups, individual legislators and civil servants. Naturally, it is impossible to review all the possible sources of advice on which ministers may draw or which others seek to foist on them. Rather, in this section we are interested in looking at the 'invited intruders' (Baum 1982) within the executive branch; those people *chosen* by the minister to help in strengthening his influence within his department.

Perhaps the most clearly elaborated institutionalisation of a selected staff serving to strengthen the position of the minister is found in the *cabinet* system in France, not to be confused with the *Conseil des Ministres*, the equivalent to the Cabinet in Britain. Each ministry in France has its own *cabinet*. The institution of the French *cabinet* is covered by a variety of legal provisions (Searls 1981: 172), including a legal maximum to the number of members (ten in most ministries). However, *cabinets* are generally larger than the legal maximum with between twenty and thirty members (Suleiman 1974: 189; Searls 1981: 172–3). The senior position within the *cabinet* is the post of *directeur de cabinet*, who is endowed with the authority of the minister. Suleiman (1974: 141) points out that the functions of the *cabinet* are to brief the minister on the implications of ministerial developments for the general policies of the government as a whole, ensure that ministerial policies are actually carried out, engaging in dialogues between the ministry and other ministries and interest groups, and coordinating and resolving conflicts between different parts of the ministry.

The French *cabinet* system has been admired in other countries, notably Britain (cf. Labour Party 1982) as a means of securing ministerial control over a department, yet how far does the *cabinet* fulfil this expectation? The fact that around 90 per cent of members of the *cabinets* are civil servants might lead to the conclusion that the *cabinet* is yet another instance of civil servants monopolising top levels of decision-making and institutionalising its power over the minister instead of the reverse. Conversely, one could argue that there would be little use in having advisers who knew nothing of the way the French higher civil service worked—who had no *Dienstwissen* in Weber's terms—since this would place them in just as weak a position as the minister in respect to his department.

In fact, it is impossible to speak of 'control' at the higher levels of the executive in France or any other country. Rather, a more accurate way to envisage the role of *cabinets* in executive policy-making is as an institution which has the potential of strengthening the role of the minister within his department rather than determining the outcome of a complex process of policy formation as the term 'control' suggests. The *cabinet* and the *directeurs*, the top officials in the ministry outside the *cabinet*, frequently conflict with each other within the policy process; as Suleiman (1974) argues, the relationship between the *cabinet* and the *directions* is one of bargaining and, frequently, conflict, but not control.

The *cabinet* system contrasts strongly with the position in Britain. It has become conventional for most ministers to call upon the assistance of at least one political adviser (for a discussion of advisers in Britain, see Shepherd 1983). As for 1983 all but two ministers in Mrs Thatcher's government had advisers, drawn mainly from the world of journalism, business and the Conservative Party Research Department (*The Economist*, 27 August 1983). Despite the importance attached to the extension of the principle of drawing upon advisers by ministers such as Barbara Castle (1980), the evidence suggests that ministerial, as opposed to prime ministerial, advisers occupy a relatively marginal place within ministries. As Young and Sloman discovered, ministers tended to use advisers to help present the ministry's policies to public and party audiences rather than actually to help formulate them—to give the dry, officially drafted statement a bit of political style. They conclude that 'if we are talking about power, power as between ministers and civil servants . . . at best [advisers] are a minor cosmetic on the granite face of the body politic: good for appearances, even for a politician's self-regard, but not likely to change very much' (Young and Sloman 1981: 91).

Indeed, the limitations to any development towards a *cabinet* system in Britain are shown up well by one apparent exception to this verdict upon the role of advisers in British ministries (see also Neville-Jones 1983). Denis Healey used a Programme Evaluation Group (PEG), comprising civil servants, some of them relatively low-ranking, as advisers when he was at the Ministry of Defence. Healey (quoted in Young and Sloman 1981: 92) argues that this group helped him formulate major areas of defence policy. Yet Healey's comments on the fate of a leading member of the PEG shows one of the main limitations on the general development of such an institution: 'he did very badly in his career for working for me. He was victimised by the Air Force for a couple of years because he'd shown loyalty to me rather than to his own service.' While there is a strong ethos within the British civil service that a civil servant should be loyal to his minister, there is also a strong ethos that binds top civil servants in an identification with the service as a whole which appears to be offended when loyalty becomes zealotry (cf. Heclo and Wildavsky 1981).

In Germany the overt increase in party influence within the personnel appointments of the 1960s and early 1970s following the Grand Coalition saw the introduction of particular divisions within the organisational structure of federal ministries aimed at providing the minister with a specialist staff, sympathetic to the minister's political objectives, to advise the minister and monitor the implementation of his policies within the department. Thus Mayntz and Scharpf (1975: 109) discuss the role of Division Z in the Interior Ministry,

Its supportive function for top executives was primarily of a political nature. The executive occasionally asked the section to help some other section or division in working out a determinate project or proposal—not in order to increase its capacity, but to make sure that the executive's political goals were sufficiently taken into account.

The degree to which such units could be found within German ministries was variable. Mayntz and Scharpf (1975: 109) also pointed to a similar unit, staffed by one man, in the Department of Housing and Urban Affairs, which was 'much too small to engage in attempts to coordinate, still less to direct the work of the divisions'. Yet such systematic attempts to incorporate political advisers into the structure of the German ministries met with great opposition from the ministries themselves (described in Dyson 1977) such that 'formal staff-line arrangements for strategic political planning have been abandoned as the conflicts of competence and of substance created by them have led ministers to doubt their usefulness.' Instead, what has developed is something closer to the British model for assistance of ministers by advisers, although this operates within a context of a more highly politicised federal civil service; the use of 'invisible planners' in the form of special personal groups outside the normal structures which operate in a 'quiet but occasionally influential manner' (Dyson 1977: 8).

Cabinet Secretaries and bureau chiefs in the United States are not short of invited as well as uninvited advice. Such invited advice can take a variety of forms, loosely classified by Meltsner (1975: 199), as advice emanating from 'staff cronies', those close to the client who offer personal friendship and advice in addition to performing more mundane tasks such as opening letters; 'program managers', those who can advise the bureau chief or Cabinet Secretary on the basis of the expertise they acquire in the process of running part of the bureau, department or agency; and 'policy analysts' who might be under contract from an executive organisation or actually employed by an executive organisation to bring analytical skills to bear upon a range of policy problems.

The fragmentation of political power within the executive system in the United States means that advisers to a Cabinet Secretary, the head of an executive organisation comprising a number of distinct bureaus and agencies, rarely constitute a group which can significantly strengthen the position of the Secretary in relation to the bureaus and agencies for which he has at least nominal responsibility. As Seidman (1980: 322) states, most Cabinet Secretaries are content to react to initiatives from others—the White House, Congress, interest groups or the agencies themselves: 'anything other than a passive approach is likely to encounter opposition from the Congress, which believes that major bureaus should be allowed to run themselves without undue secretarial interference.' Or, as Kaufman (1981a: 184) succinctly puts it: 'the Secretaries and their aides, with some exceptions, do not ride close herd on the bureau chiefs.'

The importance of advice to the bureau chiefs is underlined by Kaufman's study, which shows that chiefs requested and received intelligence, in addition to that information which was foisted upon them. The activity of receiving and reviewing intelligence occupied 'probably as much a 55 to 60 per cent' of the time of the bureau chiefs he observed (Kaufman 1981a: 45). The ability to utilise information is crucial in exercising the limited form of leadership that is found at the top of bureaus in the American system. Yet the limited nature of bureau leadership, that of 'nudging agendas, priorities and decisions' (Kaufman 1981a: 149), and the fact that the bureau chief is unlikely to rely predominantly upon one single source for such information, mean that the sort of advice received gives the bureau chief nothing resembling a collegial body to be relied upon to help formulate his policy priorities and monitor their development. Indeed, the collegial advisory body suggests a form of leadership largely absent among bureau chiefs: 'cracking the whip and personally regulating the flow of work were not ways in which the chiefs spent their working days' (Kaufman 1981a: 87).

Advice and intelligence in most forms can strengthen the role of the heads of executive departments, and in each of the four countries ministers, Cabinet Secretaries and bureau chiefs can expect advice from a wide variety of sources. The skill with which different ministers and appointees use advice and information, of course, is highly variable, and not subject to cross-national generalisation. However, only in France has the role of advisers, in the form of the *cabinet* system developed as an institutional mechanism aimed at enhancing the minister's influence within his department as opposed to the less control-oriented development of policy advice through policy analysts and the common practice of ministers seeking the advice of trusted aides on an *an hoc* basis.

COURTS AND JUDICIAL REVIEW

There are two main ways in which one might expect courts to act as a restraint upon government officials. The first is through their role as the vehicle for the redress of individual grievances which may emanate from the actions of a public body. Here courts may look to see whether a particular administrative decision is lawful and whether the individual has the right to some compensation for unlawful actions. Thus a whole host of laws, ranging from questions of child custody, taxation, planning law and property rights, are frequently the subject of litigation involving complaints against public organisations in each of the four countries. The institutions and processes for the redress of grievances against public bodies are complex and vary greatly among the four countries. In the Roman Law countries of Germany and France there is a separate body of administrative law and a specialised system of courts which hear litigation against most government agencies. In Britain and America there is generally no such distinction between civil and administrative courts. This must be qualified by the fact that, in addition to civil courts, specialist courts in the United States as well as quasi-judicial tribunals in both Britain and the US deal with individual complaints against government agencies. In addition, France and Britain each have an Ombudsman, in Britain the Parliamentary Commissioner for Administration, in France the *Médiateur*. In Germany there is an Ombudsman for military affairs, a *Wehrbeauftragte*. Although their powers and jurisdictions vary, the Ombudsmen take up individual grievances passed on to them for investigation, usually by members of the legislature. (For a discussion of redress of grievance, see Horowitz 1979; Griffith 1981; Hayward 1983; Schmidt 1983).

However, for the purposes of examining the constraints upon executive decision-making imposed by the courts, the second major form of relationship between the courts and the executive is of greater interest—judicial review. Judicial review can be of two forms; review of legislative actions and review of administrative actions. Judicial review of legislative actions is, of course, in systems where the executive dominates the output of the legislature, also to be understood as a form of review of executive actions. It is predicated upon the existence of a constitution, a higher law, according to which the legality of legislative acts can be evaluated. As such, this form of review of the actions of the executive is limited to France, Germany and the United States. Unlike Britain, these three countries have written constitutions, and courts which include in their jurisdiction cases which involve the interpretation of the constitution; the French *Conseil Constitutionnel* (Constitutional Council), the German *Bundesverfassungsgericht* (Federal Constitutional Court), and the United States Supreme Court. The second form of judicial review, and the meaning of the term understood in the British context, is that of the review of the legality of administrative actions according to the criteria of existing statutes and precedent.

The United States has a long tradition of judicial review of legislative and administrative acts. The Federal Supreme Court stands at the pinnacle of a federal court system which coexists with a state court system with a Supreme Court within each of the American states. Ever since the *Marbury v. Madison* decision of 1803 and the *Fletcher v. Peck* decision of 1810 the Federal Supreme Court has adopted the role of scrutiniser of the actions of federal and state governments from the point of view of their constitutionality. The court consists of nine justices appointed for 'good behavior' by the President with the advice and consent of the Senate. Perhaps the most clearly influential aspect of the Court's work was experienced in the 1950s and 1960s in the sphere of racial desegregation. Following a Supreme Court decision in 1896 (*Plessy v. Ferguson*), racial desegregation was declared constitutional despite the 'equal protection of the laws' part of the 14th amendment to the constitution. This was based on the grounds that 'separate but equal' facilities (e.g. schools, swimming pools, parks) for black and white were constitutional. The 1954 decision in *Brown v. Board of Education of Topeka* was the most influential of the early decisions in racial desegregation since it clearly declared the earlier 'separate but equal' interpretation unconstitutional. There followed a series of cases which reaffirmed this principle, and the Court contributed greatly to the process of eradicating some of the more blatant forms of racial segregation practised by public authorities in the United States (see Rose 1976b).

The racial desegregation issue shows how the Supreme Court in the United States has been closely involved, through its capacity to engage in judicial review, in policy-making in the United States. Moreover, its influence does not solely concern questions of individual rights (such as the racial issue) or the other individual rights issues (such as electoral apportionment and the rights of criminal suspects) on which it has passed influential judgments. In the New Deal period of the 1930s the Supreme Court passed judgment on the constitutionality of Roosevelt's economic and social welfare programmes. More recently, the Advisory Commission on Intergovernmental Relations has seen the Supreme Court as one of the major forces, along with interest groups, Congress and the executive, in the growth of government since it gave the 'green light' to a variety of programmes involving federal grants in aid to states and localities through declaring them constitutional. In addition, in some policy areas, it has moved from examining the constitutionality of certain types of administrative actions to offering positive mandates by defining the types of actions which must be pursued by federal, state and local government. In the educational field it has passed mandates giving the states additional affirmative duties towards racial minorities; and in the field of pollution it has interpreted clean air legislation in such a way is to impose greater obligations on industrial firms and the agencies which are required to monitor pollution (ACIR 1981b: 21–2).

The importance of the Supreme Court in policy-making has not only made the Court an additional focus for interest-group activity in the United States, it has also made the Supreme Court justices highly aware of the political nature of their role, since judicial review nowhere involves the simple 'neutral' interpretation and application of constitutional provisions to contemporary cases (see Hodder-Williams 1980). As the ACIR (1981b: 22) summarises:

The Court has been a powerful, if often circuitous, instrument of government growth. Over time, it has provided Congress with the mechanisms for pursuing growth, the climate for enacting growth, and the legal interpretations for implementing growth. Moreover, it has served as an arena for—and sometimes itself spawned— additional interest groups. The 'non-political' branch of government, then, has been a potent force in developing the political shape of the nation.

The concept of judicial review, in the United States, operates within a context in which the US Supreme Court is closely involved in policy-making within the executive. This does not, as the ACIR (1981a, b) study of the growth of government shows, mean that judicial review always involves a judiciary curbing the powers of a zealous executive. It is best conceived as yet another actor in the complex and interdependent world of policy-making in the United States rather than as a single 'controller' of the executive.

Of the three European nations, France and West Germany have institutions empowered to engage in a form of judicial review of both legislative and administrative actions which involves interpretation of the constitutionality of executive actions. In Britain, where there is no formal written constitution, this is impossible. If a statute is passed through the formal processes of parliamentary approval, then it cannot be declared unconstitutional in a British court. (For a discussion of the European Community Law and the European Convention on Human Rights, see Norton 1982.) Moreover, if an action by the executive is legal in accordance with the statutory powers, then a court cannot go beyond the 'natural construction of the statute' and declare actions unlawful by appeal to some higher law as is possible in a system with a formal written constitution.

Consequently, what is termed 'judicial review' in the British context is far more limited than is understood by the concept in the other three countries. It involves the interpretation by the courts of the legality of government actions within the context of existing statutes and case law. Certainly, the absence of entrenched constitutional provisions which renders impossible the judicial review of legislative actions also has important implications for judicial review of administrative actions. As Morrison (1973: 114) points out, the absence of constitutional principles in Britain in conjunction with the relatively broad grant of powers to ministers means that 'recourse to the law does not appear to be a realistic remedy to use in challenging administrative actions'. While judges frequently have wide scope to pass judgment upon the legality of government actions, Griffith argues, they have not used their discretion to challenge the executive.

This judicial activity of opposing Governments is a deviance from the norm, an aberration, which occurs most infrequently and in very special circumstances. The judiciary is not placed constitutionally in opposition to the Government, but in the overwhelming mass of circumstances, alongside it. (Griffith 1981: 227)

In Britain, therefore, it is difficult to speak of an effective check upon the legislative or administrative actions of the executive.

The French *Conseil Constitutionnel* was not originally intended as a body for judicial review of the legislative actions of the executive, rather it was originally interpreted as a means for the executive to limit the powers of the legislature. This is seen partly in its composition. Of the nine members of the *Conseil*, three, including its president, are chosen by the President of the Republic, and three are chosen by each president of the two chambers of the legislature. It is also seen partly in the original rules governing those who could place cases before the court for judgment; the President of the Republic, the presidents of the two chambers of the legislature, and the Prime Minister. Yet its role has not strictly conformed to the initial expectation. It showed its preparedness to invalidate executive proposals in 1971 when it declared unconstitutional a proposed law which gave *préfets* the power to ban certain types of political associations.

In 1974 the rules governing access to the *Conseil Constitutionnel* were changed and it became possible for the *Conseil* to be approached through petition of sixty deputies. Since 1974 there has not only been an increase in the work load of the *Conseil Constitutionnel*, but there has also been an increased preparedness on the part of the *Conseil* to challenge the laws and actions of the executive. In 1977 it struck down legislation giving police greater powers to search cars; in 1979 it declared the budget unconstitutional; and in 1981 it declared unconstitutional the level of compensation offered by the French government to the owners of the enterprises which the Mitterrand government nationalised.

A similar conclusion can be reached in the case of the German *Bundesverfassungsgericht*. This consists of sixteen justices, of whom one half are appointed by the *Bundesrat* and the other half by the *Bundestag*, in both cases with a two-thirds majority needed to support an appointment. The court itself is divided into two senates, one hearing cases concerning the freedom of the individual, and the other dealing with cases primarily concerned with disputes between levels of government in the federal system (Kommers 1976). There are no restrictions on who may approach the *Bundesverfassungsgericht*, with direct appeals to the court by plaintiffs possible.

The court has passed a number of important and influential decisions. Over the period 1951–72 Kommers (1976: 215) shows that the *Bundesverfassungsgericht* invalidated 89 provisions of state and federal law; it was responsible for banning the Marxist-Leninist *Kommunistische Partei Deutschlands* and the fascist *Sozialistische Reichspartei* shortly after the war; in 1961 it declared Adenauer's attempt to create a national television network unconstitutional; and in 1975 it declared unconstitutional the law proposed by the SPD–FDP coalition legalising abortion. In addition to passing a variety of judgments upholding individual rights against the state (see Kommers 1976), it was called upon to judge the constitutionality of two key areas of the SPD's government programme, *Ostpolitik* and workers' co-determination (*Mitbestimmung*), and has made decisions on issues concerning the discrimination against radicals in public employment, the internal structure of universities, the pay of elected representatives and the budget (see Johnson 1982b; von Beyme 1983;).

Courts have, almost by definition, some role in scrutinising the actions of government organisations in a rational-legal system of rule; where governmental powers are based upon legal definitions, then their actions can be challenged on the basis of these legal definitions through the courts. However, there appears to be a differentiation between the four countries from the perspective of the track-record of different legal systems to influence executive decision-making, either through positive mandates or declaring executive actions unconstitutional. In the United States the courts remain an important arena for policy-making, not only in questions of individual rights, but, as the ACIR (1981a, b) study shows, across a whole range of public policy issues. Similarly, in Germany, despite the shorter tradition of judicial activism in policy-making, Johnson (1982b) argues that there is some evidence to suggest that the *Bundesverfassungsgericht* has even outstripped the US Supreme Court in its influence on public policy-making. Whether or not this is the case is impossible to argue since we possess no clear criteria for measuring the relative influence of courts. However, on the basis of the frequency with which courts are invoked within political debates, the frequency with which decisions on important policy issues are brought to the attention of courts, and the frequency with which courts are prepared to challenge the decisions of the executive, one can distinguish between the US and the West German system of judicial review and the French and British. In the French case, as Hayward (1983: 141) has argued, the *Conseil Constitutionnel* has 'continued to steer a middle way, some say zigzag, between a quietist acknowledgement that the will of the people's representatives should prevail and the activist temptation of government by judges, who lay down the law to politicians prone to put short-term expediency before the protection of basic rights.' In Britain, while one can point to a form of judicial activism in interpreting the statutory rights of individuals and the executive, the form of judicial review is limited through the absence of defined constitutional principles, and even in this limited sense rarely produces challenges to executive decisions and actions.

CONCLUSION

In each of the four countries the collegial principle of Cabinet government can scarcely be regarded as an important means through which elected politicians can countervail the expertise of the permanent officials, since most policy-making is focused on the network of relationships within functionally specific groups within the executive, pressure groups and, especially in the United States, the legislature. The absence of the collegial principle in each of the four countries does not, of course, suggest that policy-making in each corresponds to a set of separate units making decisions with no reference to those outside these units. Interdependence within the executive brings cross-departmental contact, consultation and negotiation. In addition, the President and Prime Minister of each of the four countries has means of influencing decision-making in the individual executive organisations because—especially in the European countries—of the powers that they possess as the heads of government and in the United States to a lesser extent, because of the powers that they have in the budgetary process.

Concerning another form of collegiality—the appointment of advisers—the experience suggests that only in France does there exist a clear institutionalisation of a set of advisers within the ministry. Here the *cabinet* in France has some formal authority over the permanent officials outside the *cabinet*, and as a formal part of the ministry, the *cabinet* has greater opportunities to monitor and review the actions of the ministry. Nevertheless, it would be misleading to assume that the relationship guarantees the minister 'control' within his ministry; rather, at most the *cabinet* serves to strengthen the minister in the complex relationship of bargaining that characterises policy-making in France as in each of the other three countries. In Germany, Britain and the United States, ministers and Cabinet Secretaries obtain advice, but their advisers lack the formal authority found among members of ministerial *cabinets* in France.

Courts represent an institution for the redress of grievance in each of the four countries. Their success as such cannot be evaluated directly since it would require some quantification of the ratio of grievances redressed to grievances at large. There are a number of studies which challenge the capacity of the courts in each of the countries to act as adequate redresser of grievances or protector of liberties (see Gora 1977; Hewitt 1982; Hayward 1983, for examples) yet these do not permit a cross-national evaluation of the effectiveness of courts which undoubtedly varies from one area of government activity to another. However, some distinction can be made between the role of the courts in a more fundamental relationship between the law and the executive, in judicial review. In Germany and the United States the development of court activity has served to make the courts an important arena for the processing of political conflicts. In Britain and France, despite some important judicial review cases, such a role is adopted less frequently.

7 The Scope for Political Leadership

The answer to the question of whether officials or politicians rule is easy enough: both officials *and* politicians rule. In each of the four countries we have been looking at there is little dispute that officials conduct the everyday business of government—they administer social security payments and assess personal taxation levels, for example—and rule in this sense. Elected representatives and their direct nominees also rule, at a minimum because the framework within which officials work is formally sanctioned by elected democratic institutions, primarily by legislatures.

The *influence* of officials undoubtedly extends beyond this mere carrying-out of broad decisions legitimated by a legislature, for two main reasons. First, officials are frequently involved in framing policies which become legitimised by representative institutions, whether the initiative for the policy is found among officials or whether officials are involved in dealing with those, such as ministers and pressure groups, who take the initiative. No account of social welfare policy in Germany (Hockerts 1980), transport policy in Britain (Wistrich 1983), French regional reform (Grémion, C. 1979, 1982) or the growth of government more generally in the United States (ACIR 1981a, b) would be complete without an understanding of the role of officials. Second, officials invariably have discretion in the way in which they implement policies. As Hood (1976) points out, the conditions for 'perfect administration' in which there is a perfect correspondence between policy intentions and policy outcomes are never present, and almost all government programmes allow for a wide degree of discretion in carrying them out. In his classic *The TVA and the Grass Roots* (1958), Selznick shows how officials of the Tennessee Valley Authority substantively changed the role of that organisation by establishing close links with farming interests, and tended to ignore its environmental and conservation functions. This central insight—that implementation processes offer scope for implementors to shape substantively the policies they implement—has been the source of a variety of studies in Europe (Scharpf, Reissert and Schnabel 1976; Mayntz 1980b, 1983; Barrett and Fudge 1981; Dupuy and Thoenig 1983) as well as in the United States (Pressman and Wildavsky 1973; Lipsky 1979).

The precise ways in which officials can influence policy, either as implementors or as participants in making policy decisions (by which is meant the activities associated with formulating laws, general departmental programmes and granting finance for particular governmental programmes or projects) is, of course, highly variable. Strategies for exerting influence on implementation can be exerted through methods ranging from the conscious attempt to obstruct (cf. Ascher 1983) to the less conscious use of the discretion granted to 'street level bureaucrats' (Lipsky 1979). Strategies for exerting influence on policy-making range from covert withholding of information (see Sedgemore 1980, for claims of this in Britain) to more open attempts to persuade through systematic exposition of views. A detailed inventory of the strategies open to officials or used by them, a sort of 'proven means of officials influencing government policies', would doubtless require a lengthy book. Yet there is probably little mileage in such an attempt at compilation as a conclusion for a comparative study, not only because the potential means of influence are numerous, but also because strategies of political persuasion are unlikely to vary substantially across nations over and above utilising the different specific institutional structures and relationships prevailing in each. (For a discussion of sets of manipulatory strategies of influence, see Goodin 1980.)

Can comparative analysis take us beyond a statement of the trite and universal, then, and point to specific features of the bureaucratic systems of each of the four countries which are not simply summary descriptions of the institutional similarities and differences to be found among them?

THE ROLE FOR COMPARATIVE ANALYSIS

One type of generalisation from comparative analysis can be ruled out early on. It is impossible to determine from comparative analysis whether officials are more or less influential than elected representatives or their appointees. While in Chapter 1, doubt was cast on the usefulness of seeking to answer such a question, it is also dubious whether any such presentation of relative influence is possible. First, the concept of 'influence' and related questions of 'power' are notoriously controversial; there are few agreed definitions which could form the basis of any concrete assessment of relative powers of elected representatives versus officials. We have no common metric for measuring degrees of influence within a particular country, still less do we have one that can be used to compare power and influence cross-nationally. Definitions of the terms 'influence' and 'power' tend to be derived in terms of the relative simplicity of two actors, as in Dahl's (1957) famous definition: 'A has power over B to the extent that he can get B to do something that B would not otherwise do.' Such definitions are impossible to apply in the context of multi-actor relationships which would be necessary if they are to describe the relationship between a variety of different officials, elected politicians and representatives of interest groups and the legislature (see Rose 1970).

Second, an evaluation of the relative influence of officials and ministers is problematic because any such evaluation requires that we know the 'real' goals of officials and ministers uncontaminated by any modification of these goals that results from the interaction between the two. If we seek to state that the views of ministers or officials prevailed in the decision-making process, we would have to have a clear idea of what those views were, and what each side wanted from the decision-making process, in order to make such an assessment. Such an exercise is impossible, not only because it requires an ability to see inside the heads of officials and ministers, but also because it misunderstands the basis of the relationship between officials and ministers. Ministers and officials do not generally interact as if they were 'coming together for the first time rather like delegates at a diplomatic conference' (Sharpe 1976: 130). Officials have some ideas of the thinking and requirements of their ministers, and ministers acquire knowledge of the dispositions of their civil servants. A civil servant who gives advice is likely to frame it on the basis of his understanding of the needs of a minister, and a minister is likely to modify his policy preferences on the basis of his knowledge of what is, among other things, technically feasible. The *anticipated reactions* of his top officials constitute one important factor modifying his preferences. This is what Sharpe (1976: 130) terms the 'operating ideology model' of interactions between officials and their political masters according to which

the politician and the technocrat are . . . likely to have known each other over a long period and they will certainly know the context in which each operates. Each side can therefore make calculations which strike a balance between what they want and what they know each is willing and able to accept.

Thus the problems inherent in trying to compare levels of influence means that a comparative analysis cannot end up with conclusions such as 'officials in the United States are more (/less) powerful than their counterparts in France, Germany and Britain.'

Another possibility for comparing bureaucratic systems is to see whether there are distinctive contributions that officials bring to decision-making in different countries. One possible set of models is that of the four types of interaction between politicians and officials proposed by Aberbach, Putnam and Rockman (1981), who distinguish between four images of the relationship between the politician and the official. The first, 'policy/administration', is the traditional distinction, associated with Woodrow Wilson, between policy being made by politicians and officials merely carrying it out. The second, 'facts/interests', acknowledges that officials also participate in policy-making, but that they tend to stress views associated with technical facts, while politicians make broader choices about the interests served by a policy. The third, 'energy/equilibrium', envisages that 'politicians articulate broad, diffuse interests of unorganized individuals, bureaucrats mediate narrow, focused interests of organized clienteles'. The fourth, the 'pure hybrid' image, suggests that there is little distinction between officials and politicians; all are participants in the process of policy-making, and their styles, interests and values are indistinguishable: policy-making results from the interplay between actors who happen to be either elected or officials, although the precise status of the participants makes little real difference.

There is little doubt that two conceptualisations of the difference between officials and politicians, the facts/interests and the energy/equilibrium images are correct, as the wealth of evidence which the authors bring to support it make clear. One can doubt the validity of their apparent contention that this marks a stage in the development towards a system in which there is no distinction between politicians and officials since they make no attempt to explore changes over time. Nor do they establish any clear theoretical reason for postulating the different images as stages in a pattern of change over time.

Correct as it may be, this elucidation of the contribution of officials to policy-making does not take us very far by way of comparison of the role of officials in the policy process. The notion that officials derive their power from is their expertise and their contact with specialised interest groups, and the notion that the advice and influence that they offer is likely to stress the specialist views of established interests, expertise and technical facts is something that Weber among many others had assumed as a basic feature of a bureaucratic system of rule. While it is comforting to have confirmation of this, it covers only a limited aspect of the interaction between officials and politicians, and as such offers little by way of a general conclusion to a study of officials and their organisation in western nations.

The remainder of this chapter pursues an alternative form

of comparative analysis: that suggested by Weber's emphasis upon *political leadership* as the crucial variable in avoiding *Beamtenherrschaft*, or the domination by officials. Officials can be expected in any bureaucratic system to have substantial influence in decision-making. In looking at the concept of political leadership one cannot expect to derive generalisations which predict that ministers will always/ never/sometimes prevail in the policy process. Neither will this concept frame challenges to democratic government in terms of an examination of whether individuals who happen to be ministers tend to dominate individuals who happen to be officials. Such a perspective misses Weber's point about the nature of bureaucracy as a system of rule; if one were to find that those who are ministers frequently get their own way, this would not mean that they necessarily exercise political leadership. What was wrong with Imperial Germany was not that there was an efficient bureaucracy which tended to usurp decision-making. Rather, the problem of Imperial German policy-making was that there was virtually no political leadership within the political system. Bismarck had removed from the potential political leaders the prospect of having any real positions of authority within Germany. After Bismarck, the German Emperor believed that he could govern alone, yet it was the officials who governed.

What, then, is political leadership and why is it important?

THE CONCEPT OF POLITICAL LEADERSHIP

For Weber, politics is the struggle of personal power (see Chapter 2). Political activity involves building up coalitions and popular following, making compromises and being accountable for one's own ideas. Political leadership exists where one can find a politician at the apex of a state organisation. A politician has the authority and skill to assert his own preferences and priorities despite the constraints of bureaucratic government. This has been characterised by some commentators as the juxtaposition in Weber's thought of two elements; on the one hand a belief, associated with Marx, in the inevitable increase of rational-ism in the social, economic and political life of modern capitalism. On the other, a belief, associated with Nietzsche, of the capacity of individuals to assert free will.

A number of authors have assumed that Weber's beliefs about the future development of bureaucracy reflect a 'cultural pessimism' in which free will is suppressed in the 'cage of bondage' (*Gehäuse der Hörigkeit*) emanating from the development of bureaucracy as a rational form of social organisation. Certainly, a pessimism pervades much of his writing on the subject. However, Weber argues that it is possible for individuals to rise above the constraints of the 'lifeless machine'. Political leadership, precisely because it can be used to overrule the constraints imposed by the bureaucratic machine, is the only real alternative in a bureaucratic system of government to the 'pacifism of social impotence under the wing of the only totally certain inescapable power—that of the bureaucracy in the state and the economy' (Weber 1972: 836). Weber argued that the assertion of some free will over and above the constraints imposed by a bureaucratic machine did not require a *Führer*, of the sort that Germany later had; neither the principle nor the (rather divergent) practice of the *Führerprinzip* in the German National Socialist state bear any resemblance to Weber's conception of leadership. Rather, Weber under-stood political leadership to be a more limited type of activity, calling for a political leader willing to struggle to assert his ideas within the bureaucratic system: 'what was missing [in Germany] was the leadership of the state by a politician—not a political genius of the sort that you can only expect to find once in a century, not even one with a great political gift, but any sort of political leader' (Weber 1958: 324).

A bureaucratic system without political leadership will continue to function. However the decisions made within it will be subject to the logic internal to the official organisa-tions and their interaction rather than any publicly expressed policy preferences. Peters (1981: 81–2) seeks to present a picture of what, in the terms used in this book, a pure *Beamtenherrschaft* would look like. He argues that the functional divisions within bureaucratic systems would tend to

fragment control and divert attention from problems of governance to problems of organizational survival. The political life and, to some extent, the values of bureaucratic agencies are tied up in questions of organizational survival. Therefore they are almost inherently incapable of considering broad allocative and governance questions for the society. Therefore, to the extent that bureaucracies appear to be gaining in influence over policy and government, a nation will have many governments but no government.

This argument is confirmed by Diamant's (1968: 255) examination of the French Fourth Republic; ministerial instability meant that the administration 'could carry on from day to day, but it could not carry through radical innovations'. The notion that policy outcomes would, under these circumstances, be shaped by conflicts within the executive machinery, rather than through the assertion of democratically legitimised policy preferences, is similar to Rose's (1974) argument that, left on its own, a civil service will provide government by 'directionless consensus', although Peters' own variant on this term, 'non-consensual direction', shows that without the constraints of democratically legitimised government there would not even be the need for 'consensus-mongering' among conflicting executive agencies. It is not the prospect of an all-powerful authoritarian system that emerges from *Beamtenherrschaft*. Rather, it involves the prospect of perpetual *Satrapenkämpfe* in which policy outcomes are the result of private intrigues rather than public struggles for political power.

What one can expect of a political leader in a modern bureaucratic system of government is rather limited. One cannot expect that he can effect radical changes across the whole range of policies for which he is nominally responsible. And there are a number of general reasons for emphasising the limited effects that may be expected from the exercise of political leadership. First, government organisation is highly complex, and one cannot expect a

minister or Cabinet Secretary to have the time or the ability
to master the whole range of its activities and propose policy
changes across it. One clear indicator of this is the fact that
attempts to find out precisely what is going on within a
government department, such as Michael Heseltine's MINIS
in Britain or, in a rather different context, Planning
Programming and Budgeting in the United States, produce
lengthy documents of little real use to those for whom they
are written. Second, and related to this, the ongoing
commitments of government departments are built up over
periods of decades (and in some cases centuries) and it
cannot be expected that the whole range of government
activity will be shaped by one minister or Cabinet Secretary
in the span of the few years for which he or she has
responsibility for the department. Third, as Hogwood and
Peters (1982) show, the growth of government has meant a
crowding of the 'policy space'; a large number of areas of
social and economic life are already subject to some form of
government intervention. Changes in policy are rarely
characterised as government actually doing things that it had
never done before. Rather, those things that are hailed as
major political innovations frequently adapt and repackage
pre-existing policies, and make only relatively small changes
in addition. Thus, for example, they describe the creation of
the National Health Service in Britain as an instance of
partial 'policy succession' rather than pure innovation
because of the pre-existing arrangements for health care
under local authority provision.

Political leadership involves, then, the use of one's
position, gained as result of a career in politics, a career in
the struggle for political power through competition involving election within a system of representative government,
to assert the choices of the politician. It is limited in terms of
its effects. To ask how this form of leadership can be
exercised in a bureaucratic system of government is a slightly
different question from the question of whether the minister
or the official dominates in the policy process, since
ministers may not be political leaders in Weber's sense of the
term. This would most clearly be true in the case of those
presidential appointees who 'go native' in the Washington

bureaucracy, that is to say, they tend to act more as spokesmen for their departments and agencies rather than as politicians seeking to assert their preferences over those of the agency. As Weber was all too well aware, it is possible to have a *Beamtenstaat* even where ministers appear to be highly influential if ministers do not have the characteristics of the politician.

It is impossible to use this concept of political leadership to generalise how and when political leadership can be exercised in the face of constraints imposed by bureaucratic systems. It is a cliché, but nevertheless true, that some personalities have greater capacity for exercising political leadership, while others prefer to act as civil servants in all but name. Neither is it possible to go through all the ministers and Cabinet Secretaries and define which of them are 'political leaders'. What is possible within this framework is an examination of the different sources of the limitations on the exercise of leadership posed by the bureaucratic systems of each of the four countries.

CONSTRAINTS ON POLITICAL LEADERSHIP

It has already been established that political leadership cannot be characterised as the firing-off of initiatives machine-gun style with the expectation that these will guide the actions of the whole state machine as a matter of everyday routine. Yet even in non-routine initiatives, the limitations on political leadership within executive policy-making appear to be rather similar in all four countries. Not all of these limitations can be said to emanate from the civil service. However, the relationship between the civil service and external groups are at the heart of many of these characterisations. Most studies of policy-making in each of the four countries emphasise the role of *interest groups* in making policy. Chapter 5 has already examined the role of interest groups in sustaining the fragmentation of the policy-making system in the United States; in Germany and Britain the studies of 'policy styles' (Dyson 1982b; Jordan and Richardson 1982) emphasise the importance of interest-group activity in policy-making, and even in France (Hayward 1982) their role cannot be entirely neglected. Furthermore, the more one moves away from the top level of policy-making towards implementation, the more one finds the weakness of 'perfect administration' as well as the increasing involvement of groups, even in a country such as France where their influence in policy-making is generally regarded as relatively weak (see Hayward 1982). What emerges from policy-making, simply stated, is frequently the result of processes over which the leadership within the executive, whether minister or top official, has little control.

That policy-making and implementation are complex—that policy-making involves the interaction of a variety of different actors belonging to different institutions, and further that all of these factors do pose limitations to the exercise of political leadership—is beyond doubt. That they make political leadership impossible is not. One can point to examples of top executive leadership, Presidents, Chancellors and Prime Ministers, who have managed to assert policy priorities above those which might have been expected to emerge from any 'directionless consensus' resulting from the pluralistic pressures of executive policy-making. Whether one approves of the content of policy initiatives or not, some examples of Presidents and Prime Ministers offering direction to government could be found in President Mitterrand's decentralisation programmes of the 1980s, Margaret Thatcher's pursuit of privatisation, Konrad Adenauer's foreign policy, and even in Ronald Reagan's remarkable achievements in securing public expenditure cuts in certain programmes in the early part of his presidency. However, in discussing political leadership in bureaucratic systems, this book cannot look at the complex question of how Presidents and Prime Ministers can manage to sustain their policy initiatives in a complex governmental system. (For an excellent set of essays on this topic, see Rose and Suleiman 1980). Rather, this book is limited to examining the types of interaction that one can find between ministers (a term which here includes top American political executives) and officials.

At the level of the minister, too, the existence of

complexity does not preclude the ability to assert preferences above the complex array of interests which generally shape policy decisions. The fact that the admittedly unpopular Watt (who resigned in 1983 because of his unpopularity) as US Interior Secretary under Reagan managed to achieve a substantial change of direction in the environmental protection issue, the Haby initiative in French education, the economic policies of Ludwig Erhard and the education policies of Anthony Crosland suggest that the ability of ministers to give direction to their departments is not ruled out by the existence of pluralistic pressures both from within the departments and without, although these pressures have naturally meant that they could not achieve all they might have liked.

That political leadership in all modern systems of government is difficult is a truism, as is the proposition that it is possible. One can always find skilled politicians who have managed to mobilise support for their policy preferences or, at least, those of their party. Does comparative analysis, however, stop at the point of alluding to universals about pluralistic constraints on policy-making and the possibility of political leadership emerging from time to time? According to this perspective, things look more or less the same from one country to the next. This assertion is fine as far as it goes, but it is possible to point to more specific limitations on the exercise of ministerial political leadership that are different in character in each of the four countries. There are some characteristic constraints which emerge in each country. These do not preclude the exercise of political leadership; they do, however, limit the frequency with which one can expect to find a minister exercising political leadership in a bureaucratic system.

CROSS-NATIONAL VARIATIONS IN CONSTRAINTS ON POLITICAL LEADERSHIP

The institutional conditions for the exercise of political leadership in bureaucratic systems offer a means of pinpointing the cross-national differences in the institutional con-

straints upon political leadership. Political leadership consists of the coincidence of politicians at the head of a
bureaucratic organisation which is based upon a formal
hierarchy which can carry out the command of the politician.
There are two broad conditions for the existence of political
leadership, and the degree to which they are present or
absent shapes the type of limitations which in turn may
characterise the constraints upon political leadership in
different bureaucratic systems. First, the supply of political
leaders—men who have made their careers out of the
political struggle for power with the capacity to mobilise
political support for their preferred policy initiatives; and
second, the existence of a comprehensive, hierarchically-
structured governmental organisation. There are differences
between each of the four countries on each of these two
dimensions, and it is possible to use these two conditions to
pinpoint the specific problems for the exercise of political
leadership within each of the four countries.

Not all the countries in this study have processes of
recruiting ministers equally as conducive to the supply of
ministers who can be termed political leaders; a pool of
professional politicians from whom heads of government
departments may be chosen. The absence of such conditions
is particularly marked in the United States where, in the case
of Cabinet Secretaries and agency heads, there is no pool of
politicians, people who have pursued a *public* political
career, from whom appointees may be chosen. This absence
of political experience pervades the working relationship
between presidential appointees and the career officials in
Washington's 'government of strangers':

The bases of political support are highly equivocal. An executive
in Washington operates in a political twilight zone, without his
own mandate from the electorate and little capacity to gain general
public attention for what he is doing. The White House will not
readily allow him to borrow the President's reputation and
prestige, and when it does, the executive can find his acceptance
and manoeuvrability in his own organization severely constrained.
Of course, support can easily be garnered by adopting a position of
pure advocacy for the agency and its interests, but this often

divides loyalties further between an executive and the White House and narrows his possibilities for any real leadership. (Heclo 1977: 238)

The cases of Germany and France at first sight look similar, in the sense that officials are well represented in Cabinet posts, as well as in the elected legislatures. Taking a broad definition—that is, including groups such as teachers—in both Germany and France around 40 per cent of the members of the legislature previously worked as public officials. There is, however, a fundamental difference between the two countries because in Germany there is a distinctly political career, involving the mobilisation of support for the politician within the party and within legislatures, whether he be a civil servant in origin or not. Von Beyme (1983: 112) summarises the access to ministerial office in Germany thus: 'careers tend to be long and cumbersome. Access to higher executive offices needs an average of two legislatures [8 years]. Some quick take-offs in the early 1970s [so-called *Senkrechtsstarter*] remained unsuccessful exceptions.' This contrasts strongly with the French case in which the institutional conditions for this form of political leadership recruitment are weak.

Suleiman (1974: 374) argues—his important criticisms of naive 'technocracy' arguments notwithstanding—that 'it is scarcely deniable that the Fifth Republic has considerably facilitated the transfer from an administrative to a political career.' The interpenetration between administrative and political careers is such that an electoral mandate is sometimes sought after achieving relatively high office attached to the *cabinet* of a minister or the staff of the President or Prime Minister (de Baecque 1982: 66). Wolinsky's (1973: 150) analysis of French deputies presents a picture of the type of deputy who uses the electoral mandate in order to further a career in the politico-administrative system, the 'status deputy', as one who is in politics without any particular ideological preferences to further and disdainful of any form of activity aimed at generating public support or even a wide base of support within the National Assembly. Wolinsky (1973: 150) observes that 'most status deputies began their political careers in the staff of a Cabinet minister', something specific to this form of deputy. Thus there is a tendency within the French system, at least prior to the Mitterrand government of 1981, for the potential recruits to ministerial office not to have had a political career in the sense defined by Weber, but rather for them to be officials frequently using the formal procedures of democratic legitimacy as a means of status advancement without the type of cultivation of a mass following on the basis of personal values envisaged by Weber. According to de Baecque's (1982: 28) data, which includes teachers, 55 per cent of ministers in the Fifth Republic could be classed as *fonctionnaires*. In Crozier's (1964: 256–7) terms the political class has behaved according to

the same cultural traits that are at the root of the development of the bureaucratic system of organisation. [The] isolation of the political class, its fear of face-to-face relationships and its inability to solve conflicts have tended constantly to bring together the political and the administrative system whose symbiosis has become nearly perfect. But the more the political system has become bureaucratic, the less it has been able to bring to the administrative system the reform needed.

The link between parliamentary and ministerial careers (see Chapter 3) would appear, in the British case, to make Britain a place where there is a clear pool of politicians from whom a political leadership class may be recruited. This hypothesis will be examined in more detail below.

The second condition for the existence of political leadership in a bureaucratic system is the development of the bureaucratic system itself into a monocratic organisation, or rather in the case of a variety of ministries, a series of monocratic organisations over which politicians can exercise leadership. Chapter 3 pointed out that there are universal limitations to this development; none of the four countries can be said to have ministries or agencies in which the formal chain of command from superior to subordinate characterises the actual functioning of relationships within them. Chapter 3 also pointed out that it is impossible to assess whether one policy is 'more hierarchical' in terms of its government organisations than another. However, if the relevant consideration is the degree to which the formal head of the government department can influence what is done in the government's name, then one can distinguish between systems in which the government department is forced to share policy-making power with a variety of groups and individuals outside the executive—primarily interest groups and legislatures.

This is similar to Aberbach, Putnam and Rockman's (1981) distinction between 'centripetal' and 'centrifugal' systems of government. A centripetal system is one in which 'external actors can bring little leverage to bear in bargaining relations' with the executive; a centrifugal system is one in which the exercise of political leadership is far more constrained because of the dependence of the component parts of the executive upon a diverse array of external groups. It is also similar to the distinction between systems of government which are 'government'-dominated or 'sub-government'-dominated (Rose and Suleiman 1980).

Undoubtedly, interest group, as well as legislative influence can be found in all four countries, yet the discussion of groups and the legislature in this book (Chapters 4 and 5) show that some distinction can be made between systems which are more centripetal than others. In France, the weak role of the legislature *vis à vis* the executive and the status of pressure groups as 'pressured groups' suggests that the system is relatively centripetal. America is the more extreme example of a centrifugal system, with policy-making in Washington influenced in both process and outcome by the interaction between groups and the legislature in a diverse array of changing 'issue networks' (Heclo 1978).

In the case of Britain and Germany the position is not so clear. In terms of the pressures exerted by the legislature the power of the *Bundestag* is greater than that of the British parliament (see King 1976), but neither system approaches the power of the US Congress. Moreover, studies of policy-making in both systems point to the degree of interest-group involvement in policy-making. While neither system can be equated with the centripetality of the French or the centrifugality of the American system, the evidence suggests that while there is a higher degree of access of interest groups to executive decision-making in Britain than in France, the executive has the capacity to ignore many group pressures, and since the mid-1970s has done so to an increasing extent. In Germany, by contrast, studies of policy formation have pointed to a more limited scope for non-negotiable policy; studies of policy formulation and implementation (Scharpf, Reissert and Schnabel 1976; Dyson 1982b; Mayntz 1983) have suggested that the process of policy-making in urban policy, regulative policy as well as energy policy, has been severely constrained by the actions of interest groups. Support for this distinction between Britain and France as relatively centripetal and Germany and the United States as relatively centrifugal can be found in the empirical analysis of the types of contacts between top officials, interest groups and the legislature conducted by Aberbach, Putnam and Rockman, although their analysis here omits France. They argue that Britain 'fits our expectations about centripetal systems quite well'; the United States is the prime example of a centrifugal system; and Germany appears to be 'evolving in directions similar to (but not coincident with) American institutional patterns' (Aberbach, Putnam and Rockman 1981: 230).

By looking at these two dimensions we may characterise some of the salient constraints to the exercise of political leadership within each of the four bureaucratic systems. Where the structure of political careers does not favour the generation of the sort of political leader suggested by Weber, a politician schooled in the political profession of mobilising public support and compromise, then the constraint upon political leadership is one of *supply*. Where there are problems in asserting the leadership of the minister in the face of pluralistic constraints emanating from the interaction of groups and legislature with the executive, where the system is centripetal, the limitations on political leadership are limitations of *authority*, since the pluralistic consultation and negotiation that characterise everyday policy-making becomes a real constraint on the non-everyday exercise of political leadership. How does this perspective fit in with analyses of contemporary bureaucratic systems?

FRANCE: A PROBLEM OF SUPPLY?

It has long been a cliché of French politics that France is run by a relatively homogeneous technocratic élite. This élite, so the argument goes, comes from a common social background, has great social prestige, is socialised into a common mode of thought through the *Grandes Écoles*, and can maintain its position because of the indispensability of its technical training and competence for French government. Suleiman's (1974, 1978) work has done much to call this simple view into question. Social background cannot be expected to produce identical or even similar ideological outlooks, and neither can a *Grandes Écoles* training. Furthermore, the technical expertise that is gained from such a training is largely mythical, with few *Enarques* (graduates from the *École Nationale d'Administration*, the most prestigious of the *Grandes Écoles*) being trained in any specific skills that they will use in their future careers. Suleiman concludes that the French system is characterised as one in which an élite with a strong corporate identity and interest in self-perpetuation and self-preservation dominates the political and economic life of France; civil service institutions and training act as a springboard for top jobs in both the private and public sector. However, Suleiman is careful not to ascribe a clear ideological policy position to issues among French civil servants. The 'corporate identity' refers to attitudes and behaviour on issues concerned with service-wide questions rather than on specific functional policy preferences. He writes (Suleiman 1978: 247) that it would be 'difficult to pinpoint a coherent set of policies that the *Inspection des Finances* or the *Corps des Mines* are committed to within the areas of the economy or energy.'

However, there is strong evidence from the rich studies of the French civil service that, in the absence of political leadership by ministers, policy initiatives tend to emerge from within the civil service, and that the acceptance, rejection or modification of initiatives can be explained largely in terms of the frequently conflicting interests to be found within the civil service. The constraints upon political leadership in the French system do not come from a cohesive civil service with a clear set of policies that can be termed 'civil service policies', but rather, as Weber suggested in his discussion of Imperial Germany, because criteria internal to the social relations within a bureaucratic organisation, rather than the imposition of political leadership—the open struggle for power—are decisive in French policy-making. This can be seen in both the process of policy initiation as well as the processing of policy initiatives within the executive.

Catherine Grémion (1979, 1982) identifies a mobile group of civil servants—the *hors machine* civil servants—as one of the major sources of policy initiatives within French government. The *hors machine* civil servants contrast strongly with the civil servants *dans la machine* who are relatively less mobile. This latter group tend to stick to the more pedestrian career paths which accrue from membership of a particular *corps*. Those who stay in the mainstream of their *corps* career tend to develop strong identities with their *corps*, and their values and actions become structured by this identity. Above all, they are hostile towards any proposals for change which might harm the interests of their *corps*. This corresponds to the thesis put forward by Crozier (1964, 1970, 1974) and his colleagues that the *corps* system in the French executive has stifled attempts to innovate in government intervention in society and economy.

Nevertheless, the dominant role of the civil service and the *Grands Corps* within French political life gives one *corps* a position from which it may colonise top positions within ministries not dominated by the particular *corps*. The principle of *détachement* means that a civil servant can, and to be successful is expected to, spend much of his time *en détachement* in another ministry (Suleiman 1974: 241–7). This places a large number of top officials, which Grémion (1979, 1982) estimates at around one-third, in the category of the *hors machine* officials who have had the broadening experience of working outside the pedestrian mainstream career pattern of the *corps*. These top officials are 'relatively open to outside pressures and are prepared to overlook the rationality of the *corps*' (Grémion 1979: 394). The experience of mobility creates '*reseaux* of solidarity which cross *corps* divisions and are capable of exercising a dominant influence on administrative action' (Grémion 1979: 395).

The types of group that emerge as policy initiators among the *hors machine* officials are what Grémoin (1979, 1982) terms '*familles d'ésprit*'. Groups of officials 'crossing generations', *corps* and organisations who are prepared to generate policy initiatives, such as, in Grémion's case study, housing finance reform in the 1970s, on the basis of the desirability of these reforms for the system of housing rather than on the implications of a particular *corps*.

Grémion recognises, as in her discussion of regional reform, that reforms may be initiated by more conventional ministerial initiatives as well as by the *hors machine* officials, although she does suggest that *hors machine* initiatives are less likely to result in policy proposals subject to stalling or substantial modification by the entrenched interests of different *corps* or ministries. Yet wherever the initiative comes from, the limitations on political leadership in the French system derive from the pre-eminence of conflicts and constellations of interest within the civil service in the processing of policy initiatives. As Suleiman (1978: 247) argues, 'policies are judged according to their impact upon the power position of the élite'. Grémion's (1979) study of the regional reforms in the 1950s and 1960s, Thoenig and Freidberg's (1979) case study of the Pisani reforms of the ministry of housing as well as Thoenig's study of the corps of the *ponts et chaussées* all attest to the importance of *corps* interests in understanding sources of opposition to governmental initiatives. In Thoenig's (1973) study of the *ponts et chaussées*, for example, the rural entrenchment of the *corps* underpinned its opposition to urban development policies, and Thoenig goes so far as to suggest that the *corps* successfully resisted attempts to introduce motorways into France due to the perceived consequences for the *ponts and chaussées*.

There are undoubtedly different styles of policy-making in

France (see Grémion 1982), and the differences in the way in which policies are made grow the closer that one looks at the implementation end of the policy process (Hayward 1982). Two different styles have been identified by Hayward (1982) and Grémion (1982). On the one hand there is a more traditional model in which the initiatives of ministers are blocked by the powerful interests of different *corps*, and another in which a mobile and relatively open élite of administrators *hors machine* is able to innovate while at the same time accommodating the divergent interests within the civil service. Both of these models are more or less consistent with the characterisation of the major constraints upon political leadership given here; neither political leadership, nor indeed any other form of open political control, has a large role to play in the policy process in view of the importance of the constellation of interests within the civil service. Where the *familles d'ésprit* initiate policy the ministers frequently have the role of 'providing the necessary backing' for the initiatives (Hayward 1982: 122).

In all systems of government one invariably expects the officials to be involved in all areas of policy-making, and ministers to be involved in few. This is by no means a distinctive feature of the French bureaucratic system. What is distinctive about the French system is that major policy initiatives possibly emerge and certainly are processed on the basis of criteria largely internal to the administrative system. None of this is to deny that pressure groups are important, especially in implementation. Nevertheless, even this function of *articulating* pressure group demands is something over which the executive has a large amount of control.

LEADERLESS DEMOCRACY IN THE UNITED STATES

Previous chapters have discussed the absence of a pool of political leadership in the United States and the powerful pressures upon the executive emanating from outside the departments—from groups and the legislature. The problems that result from this absence of political leadership skills conform to our expectation of the relative weakness of political executives. Seidman (1980: 322) argues that appointees

rarely bring to their jobs the unique combination of political insight, administrative skill, leadership, intelligence and creativity required for the management of heterogeneous institutions with multiple and sometimes conflicting purposes. Most are content to be a 'mediator-initiator' or a reactor to initiatives coming from the White House, the Congress, the bureaucracy and the several constituencies represented by the department.

Kaufman (1981a) draws a similar conclusion. While there are two dominant models of understanding the position of political executives in the United States, one which stresses the forces producing an atomised set of isolated organisations within the executive branch and another which stresses the role of executive agencies as part of a completely interdependent executive network, Kaufman argues that a common theme runs through both these views: 'the administrative system is not fully under control.'

The official apparatus, in the absence of political direction from above is not, as in the French case, likely to lead to the dominance of officials in the initiation and processing of issues. Rather the American system is characterised by the involvement of agencies and departments in a complex web of relationships with Congress, the President, interest groups and other executive organisations in a series of 'issue networks', unstable and constituting themselves around specific issues, in which officials are better regarded as participants than in any sense 'in control'. As Heclo (1978: 105) suggests:

a somewhat new and political dynamic is being played out in the world of political administration. It is not what has been feared for so long: that technocrats and other people in white coats will appropriate the policy process. If there is to be any expropriation, it is likely to be by the policy activists, those who care deeply about a set of issues and are determined to shape the fabric of public policy accordingly.

The importance of this rather more fluid and complex form of sub-government than even that of the iron triangles (see Chapter 5) is that it poses problems for the exercise of public authority, discussed as the 'executive leadership problem' by Heclo (1978). In the United States the political leader is not, as in Weber's formulation, the person who occupies an office which has a claim to hierarchical dominance over a subordinate administrative staff. This strength, complexity and degree of integration of interest groups as 'insiders' in the policy process means that 'political administrators, like the bureaucracies they superintend, are caught up in the trend to issue specialization at the same time that responsibility is increasingly being dispersed among policy intermediaries' (Heclo 1978: 102). The consequences of this for the character of bureaucratic government are similar to the problems of the satrapic conflicts between different branches of the administrative staff discussed in Chapter 3 in which the 'courtly intrigues' of a relatively closed circle rather than political leadership determines what emerges from the interaction between them. Here, the political leader is presiding over an organisation which makes claims upon the resources of public authority (money and laws) but the organisation is not subject to the exercise of public authority.

Similarly, Wolin (1981: 251) makes explicit the relationship between group bargaining and classical conceptions of public authority by arguing that since legitimacy is something that has become associated with groups, 'public authority has no source of power peculiarly its own'. Instead, public authorities become the representatives of 'residual constituencies that . . . have not been wholly absorbed into the dominant groups' such as the ethnic and racial minorities, farm workers, unorganised industrial workers and those who are almost totally dependent upon the welfare state. 'In other words, public authority has the constituency of the powerless.' This is similar to Heclo's conclusion that

the first and foremost problem is the old one of democratic legitimacy . . . political executives get their popular mandate to do anything in the bureaucracy secondhand, from either an elected chief or Congress. The emerging system of political technocrats makes this democratic weakness much more severe. The more closely political administrators become identified with the various specialised policy networks, the farther they become separated from the ordinary citizen. Political executives can maneuver among the already mobilized issue networks and may occasionally do a little mobilizing of their own. But this is not the same thing as creating a broad base of public understanding and support for national policies. (Heclo 1978: 118)

Such creation of public understanding and support is the essence of the form of demagogic leadership of Weber's definition; it is largely absent in the United States, in which the scope for non-negotiable policies which exclude interest group bargaining and bargaining with the legislature, is limited.

WEST GERMANY: THE REACTION TO THE STRONG STATE

As discussed in Chapter 4, the German system does provide a pool of politicians who have pursued a distinctive political career within the *Bundestag*, a political party, an interest group and possibly state or local government. Furthermore, activity within *Bundestag* committees as well as the junior ministerial post of *Parlamentarischer Staatssekretär* offer opportunities for politicians to acquire familiarity with the workings of government. While we lack a study of the nature of ministerial leadership of the depth and quality of Headey's (1974) study of British Cabinet ministers (see below), characterisations of the constraints upon political leadership in Germany rarely raise questions of supply. Johnson (1982: 156) for example, suggests that political leadership in Germany has been 'pragmatic, flexible in its response to demands voiced within the political system and, at its best, decisive and public spirited'. Although Johnson also (1982: 156) detects an increasing degree of introspection within the parties which leads them to 'show signs of

becoming less concerned to a broad band of public opinion
. . . than with their own programmes and internal arguments', this refers to a potential rather than actual danger.
The contemporary problems of political leadership in
Germany can be characterised more as problems of authority than supply.

Chapter 5 discussed the importance of groups in the
German policy process. Groups are consulted, often on a
statutory basis, as is the case in other countries. Their role is
further strengthened by their ability to target their influence
on *Bundestag* committees as well as the federal executive,
although as Chapter 4 pointed out there are strong contrasts
between the American and German legislatures in terms of
their influence on legislation. In addition, as Herzog
(1982: 88) points out, interest groups play an important role
in policy formulation and leadership selection in the major
parties. The centripetality of the German system is further
reinforced by the federal structure. The federal government
has relatively few functions which it carries out without state
and local collaboration, and the second chamber, the
Bundesrat, further increases the influence of state government in federal policy-making.

Dyson's (1982b) work on German 'policy styles' shows the
importance of group pressures as a limitation on the exercise
of political leadership. In his section on health policy, he
shows the importance of doctors' organisations and health
insurance organisations in blocking reform of the health
services. While the particular features of health provider
groups arguably make their special influence on health
policy a universal feature of modern states, his other cases
show how policy initiatives become diffused by the manner
in which they are processed by the interaction of different
groups with different segments of the Bonn executive. In
nuclear energy policy, the contentiousness of the issue
resulted in an attempt to 'design procedural policies of
agenda management and consensus' and avoid raising issues
that provoked group conflict. Similarly, in economic policy-
making, 'concerted action', a form of 'corporatist' voluntary
regulation of economic policy by the state, labour and
capital, was essentially a 'convenient device for issue

management and consensus formation in the face of politically sensitive industrial problems like coal and steel' (Dyson 1982b: 39).

Similarly, Scharpf, Reissert and Schnabel (1976) point to a model of 'policy interpenetration' which emerges from the centrifugal nature of the German bureaucratic system, although their work stresses the role of divisions within the state organisation, the *Ressortpartikularismus*, of the different sectors of different federal ministries as well as the horizontal divisions between federal, state and local government. Because of the importance of these divisions, policy-making tends to produce the quest for conflict avoidance strategies in which contentious issues are isolated and set aside. The results of this process are an inability to produce policy instruments likely to have much resemblence to those desired. For example, the rationale of regional policy is that it seeks to *target* money for industrial development to particular regions. However, in the German case, the norm that conflicts be avoided produced a regional policy based more closely on a 'fair shares all round' basis.

BRITAIN: A PARTICULAR PROBLEM OF SUPPLY

As suggested above, the distinction between the centrifugal/centripetal nature of the British and German systems is a contentious one. While the discussion on Germany has tended to emphasise the evidence that views Germany as more centrifugal than Britain, this is an evaluation which other analyses (e.g. Jordan 1981; Jordan and Richardson (1982) might be taken to contradict. The issue cannot be resolved here. However, for the purposes of this discussion, locating problems of political leadership in terms of supply and authority, the contentiousness of this question is not quite so damaging as it might first appear. This is because in terms of the constraints upon the exercise of political leadership, the most enduring constraints appear to emanate from problems of *supply* of political leaders. Some of the 'ungovernability' literature of the mid-1970s (Brittan 1975; King 1975) stressed the issue of the *authority* of the state in the face of pluralistic pressures. The onset of financial stringency in the mid-1970s onwards and the coming to office of a Conservative administration pledged to an 'anti-corporatist' style of policy-making which made great play of rejecting the machinery or at least the spirit of consultation in a number of key policy areas, such as labour relations and local government affairs, showed that such pluralistic pressures were often more apparent than real. Certainly pluralistic pressures of the sort found in the United States and West Germany are found within contemporary Britain, and these pressures have in some policy areas, such as the health service and the regulation of financial institutions, sufficient power to limit the exercise of political leadership in a similar way to groups within the German and American systems. However, a more fundamental constraint on the exercise of political leadership, one which operates across a wider range of governmental functions, is a problem of the *supply* of political leadership.

At first, this conclusion may appear odd because the supply of political leaders in Britain appears to be similar to the supply of German political leadership; there is a political career, pursued through party and parliamentary activity, and one of the top positions within this career is ministerial office, with scope for junior ministerial office before actually becoming a Cabinet minister. Yet, as Headey's (1974) study shows, relatively few ministers would conform to a model of political leadership of the type found within Weber's discussion. Headey distinguishes between five different types of ministers. Policy initiators are those who promote their own policy initiatives; policy selectors are those who accept the objectives of the department and see their role as choosing between alternatives presented to them by officials; executive ministers are concerned with particular aspects of the management of their ministry and in maintaining morale; ambassadors see their function as representing the department in relations with interest groups and parliament, and minimalists conceive of their role as simply the person who signs official documents, bats for the department in Cabinet and makes sure that he does not make any blunders in parliament. Headey found that twenty-three of his sample of fifty ministers interviewed regarded themselves as 'policy initiators'. However, many of these

appeared to be doing no more than paying lip-service to a constitutional norm that said that a Minister should 'decide his policy objectives' or 'dominate his department' or 'make an impact on policy—so that everyone knows he has been there [in the Department].' (Headey 1974: 71)

A more accurate description of policy initiation, that of courting opposition within the department through over-looking 'the existing objectives and policies of their depart-ments' and succeeding in 'exacting policy programmes based upon objectives defined by themselves or their party' (Headey 1974: 191) covered fewer of the sample of fifty. He states that on such a definition 'at least nine' of the sample could be termed 'initiators'. Generally, Headey (1974: 271) concludes that British politicians are 'not qualified . . . to act as policy initiators'.

The major reasons given for this are first that British ministers are in office for a relatively short time. Although we have no strictly comparable data, Paterson (1982: 106) points out that the turnover rate of German ministers is lower than that of British ministers. The period in office for a British minister is generally between two and three years, while German ministers prior to the change of government in late 1982 had occupied their posts on average for over four years, with a median period of office of five years. Two German ministers in 1982 had been in office since 1969. In addition, German ministers are likely to have developed a greater degree of specialist knowledge of the affairs of their ministries than their British counterparts (see von Beyme 1983). Headey agrees with the argument that it takes approximately three years to see a complex policy initiative through to completion, and ministers without particularly well-defined policy objectives before they were appointed to a ministry (a clear majority, see Headey 1974: 174) require time to evolve them. The norm of between two and three years is therefore not only a problem for the minister who is appointed, say, for three years, at the outset of the formation of the government: it is also a problem for the minister taking over for the remaining period, a maximum of two years before the next election. In a similar vein, *The Economist* (22 October 1983) commented on the alternation of government posts under Mrs Thatcher's leadership: 'frequent reshuffles were the easiest way of ensuring that civil servants rule the country.'

A second reason results from the nature of party government in Britain (Rose 1974). One of the major characteristics of party government is that parties in opposition generate policy intentions which include the specification of 'not unworkable' means to desired ends which can guide the policies of the party when it comes to government. There is little incentive in the British system to produce such programmatic goals to the level of detail that may be expected in a system of party government. The specification of detailed programme objectives in controversial areas is potentially divisive. Moreover, the distance of the party in opposition from the centres of political power mean that it has little status in consultation with interest groups and is open to the charge by the government that such policy proposals are based on incomplete knowledge of the relevant facts and issues at stake.

To argue that a characteristic limitation of political leadership in the bureaucratic system of government in Britain is the supply of political leadership is not to suggest that ministers are invariably or even frequently 'weak'; at the mercy of the suggestions coming from their departments. There is too much evidence pointing to the existence of strong ministers and, above all, the importance for the officials within any government department that they have a 'strong' minister. Heclo and Wildavsky (1981: 132) argue that

civil servants invariably prefer a strong to a weak minister. . . . Given a choice between someone who passively accepts their advice and interests and someone who can effectively protect and advance the departmental interests, the Treasury and the spending departments would unanimously choose the stronger character.

Similarly, Headey's (1974: 142) questioning of top civil servants shows that

almost to a man civil servants claim to prefer a minister who puts them on their mettle, annotates their papers, poses shrewd questions in office meetings, disputes received departmental assumptions and throws out ideas for further consideration.

This conception of strength and the ability to assert an individual judgment is significantly different from the model of political leadership set out in Weber's writings. Indeed, this conception of strength is something that would be expected of a good official as well as a good minister (Weber 1958: 322–3). The strength of the strong assertive minister in Heclo and Wildavsky's study, as well as the preferred strong minister of civil servants, is that of the 'policy selector' in Headey's study rather than the 'policy initiator'. The difference between the two is not purely in the cliché that advice offered by civil servants to the 'policy selector' minister is limited and therefore the options from which the minister may choose stay under the control of the officials. There is strong evidence to support this argument in studies of the civil service (see Kellner and Crowther-Hunt 1980). Indeed, the nature of advice probably means this is invariably true, whether such options are consciously or unconsciously limited. The more important difference between even the aggressive policy selectors and the policy initiators is that the selector is responding to cues for political initiative either emanating from within the department or filtered through it rather than mobilising political support for his own initiative. As Headey (1974: 160) writes,

probably the ideal situation for a policy selector is one in which there is a large number of proposals in the departmental pipeline. These proposals may be evaluated both in terms of their intrinsic usefulness and the extent to which sponsoring them is likely to enhance the Minister's and the Government's standing.

This distinction between policy selectors and policy initiators is also important in distinguishing between the more preferred from the less preferred type of minister from the perspective of officials. Since to exercise leadership means to exert one's preferences over and above existing departmental inclinations, it appears almost axiomatic that to exercise political leadership is to court some opposition from within the department (see also Headey 1974: 211). This is supported by the preference found by Headey (1974: 153) among civil servants for policy selectors over policy initiators. While he argues that there is 'no suggestion that civil servants tend to reject non-conforming ministers like the body tends to reject transplanted organs' because of the strong and pervasive sense of loyalty in the British civil service, 'in the highly competitive worlds of Westminster and Whitehall a minister needs all the support that he can get, and it seems reasonable to conclude that policy selectors are at an advantage over policy initiators.'

CONCLUSION

In a bureaucratic system of government, such as broadly characterises the four countries in this study, political leadership is constrained by a variety of factors. The good news is that in most countries the possibility of a single, coherent, bureaucratic élite group such as might be derived from the writings of Roberto Michels, James Burnham or C. Wright Mills is constrained by the same sort of factors that could come under the heading of 'pluralistic constraints', without necessarily suggesting that pluralism is a 'good' (see Wolin 1981). The bad news is that what emerges in such a system owes less to the choices made by political leaders and more to the outcome of conflicts within the policy networks of officials and interest groups. The role that permanent officials play in these networks varies strongly; certainly the importance of the legislature in the United States plus the fact that interest groups are classed as 'insiders' in the Washington executive establishment, suggest that permanent officials have a more limited role than in France and Britain and possibly even West Germany.

The precise ways in which the constraints on political

leadership are characterised have been discussed under the broad heading of constraints of authority and supply. It is impossible to state which country is 'worse off' because of these constraints; the characteristic constraints on political leadership are quite simply different. Neither is it possible to use the categories of authority and supply to predict the frequency with which political leaders as defined by Weber can be expected to emerge. Personality is important, as is the changing social and political environment. As Heclo (1981) argues, political leadership appeared to be in many policy areas subverted by economic growth—because of a growing economy increases in public expenditure were relatively painless, and removed the difficult task of deciding priorities between different programmes and mobilising support for these priorities. If this is true, then one might expect the 1980s on *a priori* ground to witness a renaissance of political leadership since the expansion, maintenance and contraction of the welfare state each involve contentious choices between priorities.

8 Political Authority in Bureaucratic Systems

Almost universally, Weber is regarded as the innovator of the study of bureaucracy and public administration. The study of bureaucracy has, of course, moved on since the beginning of the twentieth century. What is the value of the Weberian framework for the contemporary analysis of bureaucratic systems? Its value lies in its contribution to the question of the relationship between bureaucracy and democracy and the possibilities that this offers for the study of bureaucracy cross-nationally. This issue of the relationship between bureaucracy and democracy has hardly been overlooked in subsequent analyses, yet the perspective offered here offers a sharper focus on the issues at stake in the relationship which can, in turn, be used to highlight salient differences between the bureaucratic systems of different countries.

In what ways has the study of public administration progressed since the early years of this century? There have been three dominant concerns, not mutually exclusive, in the field of public administration. The first concern is with the study of the *civil service as a social system*. Traditionally, this has involved an examination of the characteristics of civil servants, their social background, their educational qualifications, and the procedures for recruitment and promotion within the civil service (see Debbasch 1980). In addition, most interesting studies of the administrative staff as a social system also examine the values and norms within the civil service as they affect the relationships among officials, and between officials and those with whom they come in immediate contact, such as legislators, interest-group representatives and ministers. Thus, Heclo and

Wildavsky (1981) give an introduction to the cultural norms of the 'village society' of Whitehall prior to their analysis of the interaction between the Treasury and spending departments in Britain.

A second concern is with the role of the *civil service in processing issues*. Studies which look at the civil service as a social system do not necessarily adopt such a focus for its own sake, but rather use the insights gained from the social system within the administrative apparatus to help explain particular outcomes of the policy-making process. Hence Heclo and Wildavsky's (1981) study is primarily concerned with explaining how expenditure decisions are made within British government. The social system of the British civil service, its rituals, norms and conventions, are important factors which explain both its incremental nature as well as the fact that public money is subject to a form of 'private government'. Richardson and Jordan's (1979) work similarly seeks to explain how policies are made, from agenda-setting to implementation. Because the role of the civil service is important in the processing of issues, there is a tendency to focus upon the nature of the civil service and its interactions with other actors, notably interest groups, in explaining how and why policies took the shape that they did.

Undoubtedly each of these concerns is a valid and significant one, and to say that this book is not primarily about either of them is not to seek to undervalue their importance. Such concerns would simply lead one to look more closely than has been attempted here at such things as the social background of officials, the nature of their everyday working lives, the sub-culture of bureaucracy and the rituals and procedures through which relationships within the civil service and outside are conducted. The focus given by the framework used in this book is rather different from the foci suggested by these two dominant concerns. It has concentrated upon a third major issue in the study of public administration that has persisted since Weber's work: the relationship between bureaucracy and democracy.

Traditionally, the relationship between bureaucracy and democracy has been viewed in one of three ways. First, according to the 'representative bureaucracy' view, a system is more democratic when the socioeconomic and ethnic background of top government officials resembles those of the nation as a whole. Since government officials, this argument runs, have power to make or influence political decisions, it is important to safeguard democracy through ensuring that top officials are broadly representative of the nation as a whole. The fact that senior positions in the civil service are occupied predominantly by those from higher status social backgrounds (see Chapter 2) suggests that the civil services of contemporary systems are 'unrepresentative'.

A second means of viewing democracy within a bureaucratic system, a pluralistic approach, is suggested by the title of a book outlining the incremental nature of decision-making in the United States: *The Intelligence of Democracy* (Dahl and Lindblom 1965). According to this approach, democracy in public decision-making is guaranteed by the absence of centralised political authority. Officials take part in bargaining and negotiation, partisan mutual adjustment, with a variety of groups. Since the different groups can tap a variety of sources of power, such as access to congressional committees, unilateral decisions by officials is impossible and the dominance of the official is avoided.

A third way of conceptualising democracy in a bureaucratic system of government, here termed 'institutional', is to regard democracy as synonymous with the influence upon policy outcomes of a representative institution, whether it be an interest group, a legislator or group of legislators or a minister. In this sense, democratic 'control' exists to the extent that representative institutions participate in policymaking.

Each of these forms of democracy is undoubtedly valid by some definition of this rather broad term; the representative bureaucracy approach, because it emphasises the access to top policy-making jobs among a wide range of socioeconomic and ethnic groups; the pluralistic approach, because it enables a relatively (but not necessarily adequately) broad range of interests to be articulated in the policy process; and the institutional approach, because it stresses the importance of democratically legitimised institutions and office-holders in policy-making.

Finding evidence of democracy in some form or another in a bureaucratic system is unlikely to be difficult because, as discussed in Chapter 1, the development of bureaucracy was closely linked to the emergence of democratic institutions. In a broad sense, bureaucracy cannot simply be seen as antithetical to democracy. However, each of these three versions of democracy in bureaucratic systems is of limited value in meeting the central problem posed by bureaucratic forms of government: the tendency for governmental systems to develop closed policy-making networks, centred on the administrative apparatus, with policy outcomes likely to reflect relationships and tensions internal to them. In these networks it becomes difficult to assert the public authority of elective office against such pressures and tensions. In the absence of political authority, the quest for leadership becomes the pursuit of particular strategies of *bureaucratic politics*: attempting to mobilise the support of particular groups within this relatively closed system. Yet success in bureaucratic politics depends little, if at all, upon electorally-based legitimacy. Hence in a bureaucratic system there is a tension between bureaucratic politics and political authority gained as a result of the democratic struggle for power. How can democratic public authority be used to shape government activities in a direct form, and in a way for which those who possess it can be held *accountable*?

The 'representative bureaucracy' thesis is the least capable of addressing the question of how democratic political authority may be exercised in bureaucratic systems. There are a variety of general weaknesses in this body of theory (see Chapter 2). However, the greatest weakness of the 'representative bureaucracy' approach is that it confuses *sociological* or descriptive representation with *political* representation (see Pitkin 1967). While sociological representation refers to a *statistical* relationship between groups of citizens and those who govern, political representation suggests a relationship involving rights and obligations, above all *responsiveness* and *accountability*. As such, the representative bureaucracy thesis is inadequate as a statement of a proper relationship between democracy and bureaucracy; the social background of the officials has little bearing on the question of whether policy-making pursues the logic internal to executive-based networks.

The pluralist, group-based approach to the question of the relationship between bureaucracy and democracy is particularly attractive since so many studies of the four countries have endorsed it as an empirical description of the policy-making process. The problem with the approach is not primarily that, as Schattschneider (1960) and others (Truman 1958) remind us, certain groups tend to be excluded from the policy process, making any democratisation of the policy process introduced through groups highly imperfect. Decision-making invariably includes relatively few and excludes relatively many. A more fundamental problem with such an approach derives from the fact that, as a number of analysts have suggested (see Chapters 5 and 7), it is impossible to exercise *political authority* in such a system where *power* is fragmented among a number of groups, both within the executive and outside it. Indeed, in Dahl and Lindblom, this conceptualisation of a 'more or less democratic or polyarchal government' is antithetical to political authority as understood in this book; there should be 'no highest prescriptive authority in government: no agency, legislator, executive . . . can prescribe to all others yet concede no authority to any other.' In this formulation, authority is conceived of as simply one resource like any other in the process of bureaucratic politics, it is a 'counter in bargaining and other negotiation' (Dahl and Lindblom 1965: 99).

The existence of a plurality of powerful groups undoubtedly serves to prevent *Beamtenherrschaft*. However, the fact that it limits the dominance of officials through limiting political authority itself leads to two interrelated criticisms of pluralism as a normative approach to democracy in bureaucratic systems. First, through eliminating political authority it merely replicates one of the major problems of *Beamtenherrschaft*—the inability to exert human choice over a network of decision-making with a dynamic of its own. The only difference is that the network happens to include others apart from permanent government officials. Second, on a wider interpretation of the concept of bureaucracy, referring to a form of social and political organisation which extends beyond the organisation of the state itself, groups themselves may be termed bureaucracies since they have many of the features of public bureaucracies. As Weber writes, 'in character representative bodies of this sort [interest groups] tend to leaderlessness. For only those who serve the group full-time, that is to say the paid secretaries of the interest groups, will actually represent them' (Weber 1972: 175). As implied in Beer's (1977) concept of 'professional bureaucratic complexes', the specific problems that bureaucracy poses to the exercise of democratic political authority are not altered by the fact that groups happen to be privy to governmental policy-making.

The problem with the institutional approach to the nature of democracy within a bureaucratic system is that those who have received some form of democratic legitimacy may still act in the same way as permanent officials: either obeying orders, choosing between or validating the proposals of others, but not imposing outcomes upon the network in which bureaucratic politics takes place through the mobilisation of political support from outside the network. As was argued in the case of France (Chapter 7), ministers might be virtually indistinguishable from officials; they can pursue and influence policies with very little reference to any public support gained in the democratic struggle for power, and instead use their hierarchical positions as heads of ministries to influence the process of bureaucratic politics within the ministry, but they do not exert a democratically-based political authority. That such an identification of ministerial influence in bureaucratic politics with the exercise of democratic control is fallacious can be seen in the role of the British minister in the public expenditure process. In so far as ministers are successful in maintaining high levels of spending for their department, they can be argued to have influenced policy-making. Yet the goal of maintaining or increasing expenditure may not be one which can be termed the minister's own (witness the fights against spending cuts by ministers formally committed to public expenditure reductions). Moreover, the pursuit of maintained or increased levels of expenditure is one that is entirely congruent with the goals and values of top officials in spending ministries and cannot be regarded simply as an exercise of democratic political control.

The central problem that bureaucratic government poses for democracy is not that it only allows permanent officials to participate in the policy-making process to the exclusion of all others. If this were the case then one would be hard-pressed to identify any strong conflict between bureaucracy and democracy in any of the four countries since policy-making involves, to a varying degree, pressure groups, members of legislatures and ministers, among others. Rather the central problem posed by the development of bureaucracy as a form of social and political organisation is that it limits the scope for policy initiatives to be made through the exercise of political authority by politicians who have gained their authority through the democratic struggle for power. Without the ability to exercise this authority, 'democratic' forces, such as interest groups, parties and ministers, may be *involved* in the process of governmental policy-making, but they cannot give it direction for which they can be held accountable. As Long (1981: 306–7) writes,

there may be something worse than having the bureaucracy think of itself as the state. The situation may arise where nobody—legislature, political executive, pressure groups or publics—thinks of itself as the state, or in any event, identifies with the state as a primary value and a cherished, precarious, critically important institution.

The first advantage, then, of using the perspective adopted in this book is that it offers a normative conception of the relationship between bureaucracy and democracy. One possible objection to such an approach is that it is naive. Given the complexity of modern government activities, and of the relationships within and between groups and institutions involved in policy-making, it is impossible to expect policy-making to conform to such a 'top-down' model. As Kaufman (1981a: 136) suggests, only the irredeemable visionary would 'insist that the only worth-while labors in the field of public policy are those with promise of quick dramatic transformations.' However, the role of political leadership discussed in this book is a rather limited one which does not suggest that all decisions, or even all decisions of any importance, be taken by the particular type of leader who can assert political authority. Given the scale and complexity of modern government, much policy-making must in fact take place outside the purview of political leaders. Many important decisions are taken within relatively closed networks, focusing for the most part upon the executive, and the outcomes of policy processes are determined through the balance of relationships within these networks without reference to any publicly expressed preferences. In this context, the openness of the policy-making system, as envisaged in the representative bureaucracy approach, the pluralist group-based approach and the institutional approach, are desirable if not unavoidable features of contemporary policy-making. Rather, democratic political leadership in bureaucratic systems requires that leaders are capable of asserting political authority. This is neither an everyday routine nor does the capacity to exert it result automatically from high office. It is a political skill.

This conception of the relationship between bureaucracy and democracy is not, of course, unique to Weber. The emphasis upon democratic political leadership is found in the work of Gaetano Mosca and, above all, Joseph Schumpeter. Indeed, Schumpeter's (1965: 284–5) conception of democracy, that 'democracy means only that the people have the opportunity of accepting or refusing the men who are to rule them . . . [through] . . . the democratic method, viz., free competition among would be leaders for the vote of the electorate', with its emphasis upon the 'talents' of the politician and the limitations of the exercise of democratic political leadership in a modern society, borrows heavily from Weber. To point to such a conception is to resurrect rather than to innovate. Moreover, the concern with political authority is found among some contemporary studies of the United States (see Lowi 1969;

Wolin 1981). Heclo (1977: 237) identifies the weakness of political authority, the lack of 'enduring bases of political support', as one of the main features of contemporary executive leadership weaknesses in the United States federal government. What this study has shown is that the problem of political authority in a bureaucratic system is not unique to the United States.

The second main benefit of using the Weberian framework follows on from this. Since the problem of political authority in bureaucratic systems is both central and not unique to the United States, its elaboration in comparative perspective allows an exploration of the way in which the administrative apparatus of each of the four countries serves to limit the scope for political leadership. As Chapter 7 argued, the constraints upon political leadership in the United States and Germany stem from the dispersal of power between the executive and non-executive groups rather than from the permanent officials themselves. Consequently, bureaucratic politics in these two countries are less dominated by permanent officials within the executive than in France and Britain. Moreover, the approach allows one to explore the degree to which different countries vary according to the conditions which appear to affect their capacity to generate the form of leadership required to assert political authority.

Little is served by adding to fears of bureaucracy as a 'raging pandemic' (Kaufman 1981b) or by offering a critique of bureaucracy which empathises with K., the hero of Kafka's *The Castle*, in which the individual is pushed around by an anonymous, and apparently monolithic organisation which can control every feature of an individual's life. Neither does the search for evidence of important decisions which appear to have been taken by permanent officials without the involvement of any outsiders, or even of 'bureaucratic sabotage' of a minister's wishes, take us very far in understanding the nature of bureaucratic government. In fact, if these considerations reflect one's fears about bureaucracy, then the evidence suggests that there is little to worry about in any of the four western nations examined here. The administrative apparatus is manned admittedly for the most part by people who are far from household names, but it is nowhere a monolith, rarely engages in overt sabotage, and routinely consults outside interests when it is involved in policy-making.

Bureaucracy is both a desirable and unavoidable form of social and political organisation. Consequently, such fears display a helplessness and negativism which are unlikely to be redressed by any conceivable measure. The real dangers of bureaucratic government are more complex and less immediate. The notion that 'politics has gone underground' (Richardson and Jordan 1979: 191) appears to incite greater resourcefulness in the academic understanding of the 'murky and complex' world of policy-making rather than to generate concern that what was once regarded as a defining feature of political activity, its publicness (Wolin 1961; Crick 1964), has been lost somewhere along the way. Bureaucratic systems without political leadership do not necessarily produce bad, inefficient, arbitrary or even illiberal government. They are merely systems over which there is no *public* control.

Bibliography

Aberbach, J.D. (1979) 'Changes in congressional oversight', in C.H. Weiss and A.H. Barton (eds), *Making Bureaucracies Work*, Beverly Hills: Sage.

Aberbach, J.D., Putnam, R.D. and Rockman, B.A. (1981) *Bureaucrats and Politicians in Western Democracies*, Cambridge, Mass.: Harvard University Press.

Albertin, L. (1983) 'Les rapports entre les Länder et les communes en Allemagne Fédérale', in A. Mabileau (ed.), *Les Pouvoirs locaux à l'épreuve de la décentralisation*, Paris: Pedone.

Albrow, M. (1970) *Bureaucracy*, London: Macmillan.

Andrews, W.G. (1981) 'The collective political executive under the Gaullists', in W.G. Andrews and S. Hoffman (eds), *The Fifth Republic at Twenty*, Albany, NY: State University of New York Press.

Andrews, W.G. (1983) *Presidential Government in Gaullist France*, Albany, NY: State University of New York Press.

Ascher, K. (1983) 'The politics of administrative opposition—council house sales and the right to buy', *Local Government Studies*, 9, 2: 12–20.

Ashford, D.E. (1982) *British Dogmatism and French Pragmatism*, London: Allen & Unwin.

Baestlein, A. *et al.* (1978) 'State governments and local development planning in the Federal Republic of Germany', in K. Hanf and F.W. Scharpf (eds), *Interorganizational Policy-Making*, Beverly Hills and London: Sage.

Barker, A. (ed.) (1982) *Quangos in Britain*, London: Macmillan.

Barker, E. (1944) *The Development of Public Services in Western Europe 1660–1930*, London: Oxford University Press.

Barnard, C. (1951) *The Functions of the Executive*, Cambridge, Mass.: Harvard University Press.

Barnett, J. (1981) *Inside the Treasury*, London: André Deutsch.

Barrett, S. and Fudge, C. (eds) (1981) *Policy and Action*, London: Methuen.

Baum, H.S. (1982) 'The advisor as invited intruder', *Public Administration Review*, 42, 6: 546–52.

Becquart-Leclercq, J. (1978) *Les Paradoxes du pouvoir local*, Paris: Presses de la Fondation Nationale des Sciences Politiques.

Beer, S.H. (1973) 'The modernization of American federalism', *Publius*, Fall: 49–95.

Beer, S.H. (1977) 'Political overload and federalism', *Polity*, 10, 1: 5–17.

Beer, S.H. (1978) 'In search of a new public philosophy', in A. King (ed.), *The New American Political System*, Washington, DC: American Enterprise Institute.

Beer, S.H. (1980) 'British pressure groups revisited: pluralistic stagnation from the fifties to the seventies', *Public Administration Bulletin*, 32, 5–16.

Beer, S.H. (1982) *Britain Against Itself*, London: Faber & Faber.

Berman, L. (1979) *The Office of Management and Budget and the Presidency 1921–1979*, Princeton, NJ: Princeton University Press.

Bertram, J. (1967) *Staatspolitik und Kommunalpolitik*, Stuttgart: Kohlhammer.

Birnbaum, P. (1982) *The Heights of Power*, Chicago: University of Chicago Press.

Birrell, W.D. and Murie, A. (1980) *Policy and Government in Northern Ireland*, Dublin: Gill & Macmillan.

Blau, P.M. and Meyer, M.W. (1971) *Bureaucracy in Modern Society*, New York: Random House.

Blom-Cooper, L. (1982) 'The new face of judicial review: administrative changes in Order 53', *Public Law*, Summer: 250–61.

Boaden, N. (1971) *Urban Policy-Making*, London: Cambridge University Press.

Bodiguel, J.-L. (1983) 'A French-style spoils system', *Public Administration*, 61, 3: 295–9.

Braunthal, G. (1965) *The Federation of German Industry in Politics*, Ithaca, NY: Cornell University Press.

Brazier, R. (1983) 'Further reforms of Commons procedures', *Public Law*, Spring: 16–19.

Brittan, S. (1975) 'The economic consequences of democracy', *British Journal of Political Science*, 5, 2: 129–59.

Brown, R.G. (1983) 'Party and bureaucracy from Kennedy to

Reagan', *Political Science Quarterly*, 97, 2: 279–94.

Bulpitt, J. (1983) *Territory and Power in the United Kingdom*, Manchester: Manchester University Press.

Burnham, J. (1962) *The Managerial Revolution*, Harmondsworth: Penguin.

Caiden, N. (1982) 'The myth of the annual budget', *Public Administration Review*, 6: 516–23.

Castle, B. (1980) *The Castle Diaries 1974–76*, London: Weidenfeld & Nicolson.

Cater, D. (1964) *Power in Washington*, New York: Random House.

Civil Service Commission (1981) *Annual Report 1981*, Basingstoke: Civil Service Commission.

Clark, T.B. (1981) 'Can Reagan break the iron triangle? The President takes on the iron triangles and so far holds his own', *National Journal*, 13, 28 March.

Cohen, S. (1980) *Les Conseillers du President*, Paris: Presses Universitaires de France.

Collella, C.C. and Beam, D.R. (1981) 'Political dynamics of intergovernmental policy-making', in J.J. Hanus (ed.), *The Nationalization of State Government*, Lexington, Mass.: D.C. Heath.

Copeman, H. (1981) 'Analysing public expenditure' (2 parts), *Journal of Public Policy*, 1, 3 and 4: 289–306; 481–99.

Crick, B. (1964) *In Defence of Politics*, Harmondsworth: Penguin.

Crossman, R.H.S. (1983) 'Introduction' to W. Bagehot, *The English Constitution*, London: Collins.

Crossman R.H.S. (1975) *Diaries of a Cabinet Minister*, London: Jonathan Cape.

Crozier, M. (1964) *The Bureaucratic Phenomenon*, London: Tavistock.

Crozier, M. (1970) *La Societée bloquée*, Paris: Le Seuil.

Crozier, M. (1980) *On ne change pas la societée par decret*, Paris: Grasset.

Crozier, M. and Thoenig, J.-C. (1976) 'The regulation of complex organized systems', *Administrative Science Quarterly*, 21, 4: 547–70.

Crozier, M. *et al.* (1974) *Où va l'administration française?* Paris: Les Editions d'Organisation.

Dahl, R.A. (1957) 'The concept of power', *Behavioral Science*, 2: 201–15.

Dahl, R.A. and Lindblom C.E. (1965) *The Intelligence of Democracy*, New York: Free Press.

Darbel, A. and Schnapper, D. (1969) *Le Système administratif*, Paris: Mouton.

Dearlove, J. (1973) *The Politics of Policy in English Local Government*, London: Cambridge University Press.

de Baecque, F. (1982) 'L'interpénétration des personnels administratifs et politiques', in F. de Baecque and J.-L. Quermonne (eds), *Administration et politique sous la cinquième republique*, Paris: Presses de la Fondation Nationale des Sciences Politiques.

Debbasch, C. (ed.) (1980) *La Fonction publique en Europe*, Paris: CNRS.

Dell, E. (1980) 'Collective responsibility: fact, fiction or façade?', in Royal Institute of Public Administration (ed.), *Policy and Practice. The Experience of Government*, London: RIPA.

Dempster, M.A.H. and Wildavsky, A. (1979) 'On change: or, there is no magic size for an increment', *Political Studies*, 27: 371–89.

Derthick, M. (1970) *The Influence of Federal Grants: Public Assistance in Massachusetts*, Cambridge, Mass.: Harvard University Press.

Diamant, A. (1962) 'The bureaucratic model: Max Weber rejected, rediscovered, reformed', in F.L. Headey and S.L. Stokes (eds), *Papers in Comparative Public Administration*, Ann Arbor, Michigan: University of Michigan Institute of Public Administration.

Diamant, A. (1968) 'Tradition and innovation in French administration', *Comparative Political Studies*, 1, 2: 251–74.

Djilas, M. (1957) *The New Class*, London: Thames & Hudson.

Dogan, M. (1979) 'How to become a minister in France: Career pathways 1870–1978', *Comparative Politics*, 12, 1: 1–26.

Downs, S. (1983) 'Select committees in the House of Commons: an ineluctable development', Hull: University of Hull Papers in Politics no. 32.

Drewry, G. (1983) 'The national audit act: half a loaf?' *Public Law*, Winter, 531–7.

Dunleavy, P. and Rhodes, R.A.W. (1983) 'Beyond Whitehall', in H.M. Drucker *et al.* (eds), *Developments in British Politics*, London: Macmillan.

Dupuy, F. and Thoenig, J.-C. (1983) *Sociologie de l'administration française*, Paris: Armand Colin.

Dyson, K. (1977) 'The West German party book administration: an evaluation', *Public Administration Bulletin*, 25: 3–23.

Dyson, K. (1980) *The State Tradition in Western Europe*, Oxford:

Martin Robertson.

Dyson, K. (1982a) 'The politics of economic recession in western Germany', in A.W. Cox (ed.), *Politics, Policy and the European Recession*, London: Macmillan.

Dyson, K. (1982b) 'West Germany: The search for a rationalist consensus', in J. Richardson (ed.) *Policy Styles in Western Europe*, London: Allen & Unwin.

Eisenstadt, S.N. (1956) 'Political struggles in bureaucratic societies, *World Politics*, 9, 1: 15–36.

Elazar, D.J. (1962) *The American Partnership*, Chicago: University of Chicago Press.

Elliott, M. (1981) 'The role of law in central–local relations', London: Social Science Research Council.

Ellwein, T. (1973) *Das Regierungssystem der Bundesrepublik Deutschland*, Opladen: Westdeutscher Verlag.

Ellwein, T. (1974) 'Die grossen Interessenverbände und ihr Einfluss', in R. Loewenthal and H.-P. Scharz (eds), *Die Zweite Republik*, Stuttgart: Seewald.

Eschenburg, T., (1963) *Herrschaft der Verbände?*, 2nd edn, Stuttgart: Deutsche Verlagsanstalt.

Escoube, P. (1980) 'Les grands corps administratifs', in M. Boucher (ed.), *La Fonction publique*, Cahiers Français, 197: 28–31.

Fenno, R. (1959) *The President's Cabinet*, Cambridge, Mass.: Harvard University Press.

Finer, H. (1945) 'Critics of bureaucracy', *Political Science Quarterly*, 60, 1, 100–12.

Flegman, V. (1980) *Called to Account*, Farnborough, Hants.: Gower.

Fogelson, R. (1967) *Fragmented Metropolis*, Cambridge, Mass.: Harvard University Press.

Frears, J.R. (1981) 'Parliament in the Fifth Republic', in W.G. Andrews and S. Hoffman (eds), *The Fifth Republic at Twenty*, Albany, NY: State University of New York Press.

Freeman, J.L. (1965) *The Political Process. Executive Bureau–Legislative Committee Relations*, New York: Random House.

Fulton Committee (1968) *The Civil Service. Report of the Committee 1966–68*, Cmnd 3638, London: HMSO.

Garrett, J. (1980) *Managing the Civil Service*, London: Heinemann.

Giddens, A. (1971) *Capitalism and Modern Social Theory*, London: Cambridge University Press.

Gneist, R. von (1891) *The History of the English Constitution*,

London: Clowes.

Goodin, R.E. (1980) *Manipulatory Politics*, New Haven and London: Yale University Press.

Gora, J.M. (1977) *Due Process of Law*, Stokie, Ill.: Natural Textbook Company.

Green, D. (1981) 'The budget and the plan', in P.G. Cerny and M.A. Schain (eds), *French Politics and Public Policy*, London: Methuen.

Grémion, C. (1979) *Profession: decideurs*, Paris: Gauthier-Villars.

Grémion, C. (1982) 'Le milieu decisionnel central', in F. de Baecque and J.-L. Quermonne (eds), *Administration et politique sous la Cinquième Republique*, Paris: Presses de la Fondation Nationale des Sciences Politiques.

Grémion, P. (1970) 'Introduction à une étude du système politico-administratif local', *Sociologie du Travail*, 1, 51–73.

Grémion, P. (1976) *Le Pouvoir peripherique*, Paris: Editions du Seuil.

Griffith, J.A.G. (1966) *Central Departments and Local Authorities*, London: Allen and Unwin.

Griffith, J.A.G. (1974) *Parliamentary Scrutiny of Government Bills*, London: PEP.

Griffith, J.A.G. (1977) 'Standing committees in the House of Commons', in S.A. Walkland and M. Ryle (eds), *The Commons in the 70s*, Glasgow: Fontana.

Griffith, J.A.G. (1981) *The Politics of the Judiciary*, 2nd edn, Glasgow: Fontana.

Grodzins, M. (1960) 'The federal system', in The President's Commission on National Goals (ed.), *Goals for Americans*, Englewood Cliffs, NJ: Prentice Hall.

Groupe des Specialistes des Études Parlementaires (1980) 'The French parliament and the economy', in D. Coombes and S.A. Walkland (eds), *Parliaments and Economic Affairs*, London: Heinemann.

Halpern, O. and Oury, J.-M. (1980) 'Les grands corps techniques', in M. Boucher (ed.), *La Fonction publique*, Cahiers Français, 197: 32–6.

Hanson, A.H. and Walles, M. (1975) *Governing Britain*, Glasgow: Fontana.

Hanus, J.J. (ed.) (1981) *The Nationalization of State Government*, Lexington, Mass.: D.C. Heath.

Hartley, O.A. (1971) 'The relationship between central and local authorities', *Public Administration*, 49, 439–56.

Hartman, R.W. (1982) 'Congress and budget-making', *Political*

Science Quarterly, 97, 3: 381–402.

Havermann, J. (1981) 'Inside the Reagan administration', *National Journal*, 25 April.

Hayward, J.E.S. (1982) 'Mobilizing private interests in the service of public ambitions: the salient element in the dual French policy style', in J. Richardson (ed.), *Policy Styles in Western Europe*, London: Allen & Unwin.

Hayward, J.E.S. (1983) *The One and Indivisible French Republic*, 2nd edn, London: Weidenfeld & Nicolson.

Headey, B. (1974) *British Cabinet Ministers*, London: Allen & Unwin.

Heclo, H. (1977) *A Government of Strangers*, Washington, DC: Brookings Institution.

Heclo, H. (1978) 'Issue networks and the executive establishment', in A. King (ed.), *The New American Political System*, Washington, DC: American Enterprise Institute.

Heclo, H. (1981) 'Towards a new welfare state', in P. Flora and A.J. Heidenheimer (eds), *The Development of Welfare States in Europe and America*, New Brunswick, NJ: Transaction Books.

Heclo, H. (1983) 'One executive branch or many?', in A. King (ed.), *Both Ends of the Avenue*, Washington, DC: American Enterprise Institute.

Heclo, H. and Salaman, L. (eds) (1981) *The Illusion of Presidential Government*, Boulder, Colorado: Westview Press.

Heclo, H. and Wildavsky, A. (1981) *The Private Government of Public Money*, London: Macmillan.

Helmer, J. (1981) 'The presidential office: velvet fist in an iron glove', in H. Heclo and L. Salaman (eds), *The Illusion of Presidential Government*, Boulder, Colorado: Westview Press.

Hewart, the Rt Hon. Lord Hewart of Bury (1929) *The New Despotism*, London: Benn.

Hewitt, P. (1982) *The Abuse of Power*, Oxford: Martin Robertson.

Hockerts, H.G. (1980) *Sozialpolitische Entscheidungen im Nachkriegsdeutschland*, Stuttgart: Clett Cotta.

Hodder-Williams, R. (1980) *The Politics of the United States Supreme Court*, London: Allen & Unwin.

Hogwood, B.W. (1982) 'In search of accountability: the territorial dimensions of industrial policy', *Public Administration Bulletin*, 38: 22–39.

Hogwood, B.W. and Peters, B.G. (1982) *Policy Dynamics*, Brighton: Wheatsheaf.

Hood, C.C. and Dunsire, A. (1981) *Bureaumetrics*, Farnborough,

Hants: Gower.

Horowitz, D.L. (1979) 'The courts as monitors of the bureaucracy', in C.H. Weiss and A.H. Barton (eds), *Making Bureaucracy Work*, Beverly Hills and London: Sage.

Ingram, H. (1977) 'Policy implementation through bargaining: the case of federal grants in aid', *Public Policy*, 25: 199–525.

Institute of Public Administration (1948) 'Central control of local authorities', *Public Administration*, 26: 118–22.

Jacoby, H. (1973) *The Bureaucratisation of the World*, Berkeley, Cal.: University of California Press.

Johnson, N. (1976) *Government in the Federal Republic of Germany*, Oxford: Pergammon.

Johnson, N. (1977) 'Select committees as tools of parliamentary reform', in S.A. Walkland and M. Ryle (eds), *The Commons in the 1970s*. Glasgow: Fontana.

Johnson, N. (1979) 'Committees in the West German *Bungestag*', in J.D. Lees and M. Shaw (eds), *Committees in Legislatures: a comparative analysis*, Oxford: Martin Robertson.

Johnson, N., (1982a) 'Parties and the conditions of political leadership', in H. Doering and G. Smith (eds), *Party Government and Political Culture in Western Germany*, London: Macmillan.

Johnson, N. (1982b) 'The interdependence of law and politics: judges and the constitution in West Germany', *West European Politics*, 5, 3: 236–52.

Jordan, A.G. (1981) 'Iron triangles, woolly corporatism or elastic nets: images of the policy process', *Journal of Public Policy*, 1, 1: 95–123.

Jordan, A.G. and Richardson J. (1982) 'The British policy style or the logic of negotiation?', in J. Richardson (ed.), *Policy Styles in Western Europe*, London: Allen & Unwin.

Kaack, H. (1971) *Geschichte und Struktur des deutschen Parteiensystems*, Opladen: Westdeutscher Verlag.

Kaltefleiter, W. (1976) 'The recruitment market of the German political elite', in H.E. Eulau and M.M. Czudnowski (eds), *Elite Recruitment in Democratic Polities*, New York: Halsted Press.

Kaufman, H. (1981a) *The Administrative Behavior of Federal Bureau Chiefs*, Washington, DC: Brookings Institution.

Kaufman, H. (1981b) 'Fear of bureaucracy: a raging pandemic', *Public Administration Review*, 41, 1: 1–9.

Keeler, J. (1981) 'The corporatist dynamic of agricultural modernisation in the Fifth Republic', in W.G. Andrews and S.

Hoffman (eds), *The Fifth Republic at Twenty*, Albany, NY: State University of New York Press.

Kellner, P. and Lord Crowther-Hunt (1980) *The Civil Servants*, London: Futura.

Kesselman, M. (1970) *The Ambiguous Consensus*, New York: Alfred Knopf.

King, A. (1975) 'Overload: problems of governing in the 1970s', *Political Studies*, 23, 2/3: 284–96.

King, A. (1976) 'Models of executive–legislative relations. Britain, France and West Germany', *Legislative Studies Quarterly*, 1, 1: 37–65.

Koenig, K. (1983) 'Education and training for the public service in the Federal Republic of Germany', *International Review of Administrative Sciences*, 49, 2: 204–9.

Kogan, M., Crosland, A. and Boyle, E. (1971) *The Politics of Education*, Harmondsworth: Penguin.

Kommers, D. (1976) *Judicial Politics in West Germany*, Beverly Hills: Sage.

Labour Party (1982) *Labour's Programme 1982*, London: Labour Party.

Laurens, A. (1980) *Le Métier politique*, Paris: Editions Alain Moreau.

Le Grand, J. (1982) *A Strategy of Equality*, London: Allen & Unwin.

Lipsky, M. (1979) *Street Level Bureaucracy*, New York: Russell Sage Foundation.

Long, N.E. (1981) 'The SES and the public interest', *Public Administration Review*, 41, 3: 305–12.

Loquet, P. (1981) *Les Commissions parlementaires permanentes de la Vᵉ république*. Paris: Presses Universitaires de France.

Lord, G. (1972) *The French Budgetary Process*, Berkeley, Cal.: University of California Press.

Lowi, T.J. (1969) *The End of Liberalism*, New York: Norton.

Lowi, T.J. (1979) 'The state of cities in the Second Republic', in J.P. Blair and D. Nachmias (eds), *Fiscal Retrenchment and Urban Policy*, Beverly Hills: Sage.

Lynn, N.B. and Vaden, R.E. (1979) 'Bureaucratic response to civil service reform', *Public Administration Review*, 39, 4: 333–43.

Mabileau, A. (ed.) (1983) *Les Pouvoirs locaux a l'épreuve de la décentralisation*, Paris: Pedone.

Mackie, T.T. and Hogwood, B.W. (1983) 'Cabinet committees in executive decision-making', Glasgow: University of Strathclyde, *Studies in Public Policy*, no. 111.

Marlan, R.L., (1967) 'Local government: an embarrassment of riches', in J.W. Foster (ed.), *The 50 States and their Local Governments*, New York: Knopf.

Masclet, J.-C. (1979) *Le Rôle du deputé et ses attachés institutionelles sous la Ve république*, Paris: Librairie Générale de Droit et de Jurisprudence.

Mastias, J. (1980) *Le Sénat de la Ve république: réforme et renouveau*, Paris: Economica.

Mayntz, R. (1965) 'Max Webers Idealtypus de Bürokratie und die Organisationssoziologie', *Kölner Zeitschift für Soziologie und Sozialpsychologie*, 17, 493–502.

Mayntz, R. (1978) *Soziologie der Öffentlichen Verwaltung*, Heidelberg: Müller.

Mayntz, R. (1980a) 'Executive leadership in Germany. Dispersal of Power or *Kanzlerdemokratie?*', in R. Rose and E.N. Suleiman (eds), *Presidents and Prime Ministers*, Washington, DC: American Enterprise Institute.

Mayntz, R. (ed.) (1980b) *Implementation Politischer Programme I*, Königstein: Hain.

Mayntz, R. (ed.) (1983) *Implementation Politischer Programme II*, Opladen: Westdeutscher Verlag.

Mayntz, R. and Scharpf, F.W. (1975) *Policy-Making in the German Federal Bureaucracy*, Amsterdam: Elsevier.

Meltsner, A. (1975) *Policy Analysis in the Bureaucracy*, Berkeley, Cal.: University of California Press.

Mény, Y. (1983) 'Permanence and change: the relations between central government and local authorities in France', *Government and Policy*, 1, 1: 17–28.

Meyer, J.P. (1964) *Max Weber and German Politics*, 2nd edn, London: Faber & Faber.

Mezey, M.L. (1979) *Comparative Legislatures*, Durham, North Carolina: Duke University Press.

Moe, R.C. and Teel, S.C. (1970) 'Congress as policy-maker: a necessary reappraisal', *Political Science Quarterly*, 85, 3: 443–70.

Morrison, F.L. (1973) *Courts and the Political Process in England*, Beverly Hills: Sage.

Nelson, M. (1982) 'A short, ironic history of American national bureaucracy', *Journal of Politics*, 44, 3: 746–78.

Neville-Jones, P. (1983) 'The continental cabinet system', *The Political Quarterly*, 53, 3: 232–42.

Norton, P. (1981) *The Commons in Perspective*, Oxford: Martin Robertson.

Norton, P. (1982) *The Constitution in Flux*, Oxford: Martin Robertson.

Norton, P. (1983) 'Parliament and policy', Paper presented to the American Political Science Association, Chicago, August.

Page, E. (1980) 'Comparing local expenditure: lessons from a multi-national state', University of Strathclyde Studies in Public Policy no. 60.

Page, E. (1982) 'Laws and orders in central–local government relations', University of Strathclyde Studies in Public Policy no. 103.

Page, E. (1983) 'La marginalisation des élites politiques locales en Grande-Bretagne', in A. Mabileau (ed.) *Les Pouvoirs locaux a l'épreuve de la décentralisation*, Paris: Pedone.

Paterson, W.E. (1982) 'Problems of party government in West Germany', in H. Doering and G. Smith (eds), *Party Government and Political Culture in Western Germany*, London: Macmillan.

Peters, B.G. (1981) 'The problem of bureaucratic government, *Journal of Politics*, 43, 1: 56–82.

Pitkin, H.F. (1967) *The Concept of Representation*, Berkeley, Cal.: University of California Press.

Pitt, D. and Smith, B.C. (1981) *Government Departments: an Organisational Perspective*, London: Routledge.

Pliatzky, Sir L. (1980) *Getting and Spending*, Oxford: Basil Blackwell.

Polsby, N. (1978) 'Presidential cabinet-making', *Political Science Quarterly*, 93, 1: 15–25.

Pressman, J. and Wildavsky, A. (1973) *Implementation*, Berkeley: University of California Press.

Putnam, R.D. (1973) 'The political status of senior civil servants in Western Europe. A preliminary analysis', *British Journal of Political Science*, 3, 3: 257–90.

Rausch, H. (1976) *Bundestag und Bundesregierung*, Beck: Munich.

Reissert, B. (1980) 'Federal and state transfers to local government in the Federal Republic of Germany: a case of political immobility', in D.E. Ashford (ed.), *Financing Urban Government in the Welfare State*, London: Croom Helm.

Rhodes, R.A.W. (1981) *Control and Power in Central–Local Government Relationships*, Farnborough, Hants: Gower.

Rhodes, R.A.W. (1983) 'Can there be a national community of

local government.' *Local Government Studies*, 9, 6: 17–37.

Richardson, J.J. (ed.) (1982) *Policy Styles in Western Europe*, London: Allen & Unwin.

Richardson, J.J. and Jordan, A.G. (1979) *Governing Under Pressure*, Oxford: Martin Robertson.

Ridley, F.F. (ed.) (1968) *Specialists and Generalists. A Comparative Perspective*, London: Allen & Unwin.

Ridley, F.F. (1983) 'Career service: a comparative perspective on civil service promotion', *Public Administration*, 62(2): 179–96.

Riggs, F. (1969) *Bureaucratic Politics in Comparative Perspective*, Honolulu: Social Science Research Institute.

Ring, P.S. and Perry, J.L. (1983 'Reforming the upper levels of the bureaucracy: a longitudinil study of the senior executive service', *Administration and Society*, 15, 1: 119–43.

Rose, R. (1970) *People in Politics*, London: Faber & Faber.

Rose, R. (1974) *The Problem of Party Government*, Harmondsworth: Penguin.

Rose, R. (1976a) 'On the priorities of government: a developmental analysis of public policies, *European Journal of Political Research*, 4, 2: 247–89.

Rose, R. (1976b) 'The priorities of citizenship in the Deep South and Northern Ireland', *Journal of Politics*, 38, 2: 247–91.

Rose, R. (1980a) 'British government. The Job at the top', in R. Rose and E.N. Suleiman (eds), *Presidents and Prime Ministers*, Washington, DC: American Enterprise Institute.

Rose, R. (1980b) 'Governments against sub-governments. A European perspective on Washington', in R. Rose and E.N. Suleiman (eds), *Presidents and Prime Ministers*, Washington, DC: American Enterprise Institute.

Rose, R. (1981) 'The political status of higher civil servants in Britain', Glasgow: University of Strathclyde Studies in Public Policy no. 92.

Rose, R. (1982) *Understanding the United Kingdom*, London: Longman.

Rose, R. (1983) 'The role of laws in comparative perspective', *Studies in Public Policy*, 106, Glasgow: University of Strathclyde, Centre for the Study of Public Policy.

Rose, R. (ed.) (forthcoming) *Public Employment in Western Nations*, London: Cambridge University Press.

Rose, R. and Page, E. (1982) 'Chronic instability in scal systems', in R. Rose and E. Page (eds), *Fiscal Stress in Cities*, London: Cambridge University Press.

Rose, R. and Peters, B.G. (1978) *Can Government Go Bank-*

rupt?, London: Macmillan.

Rose, R. and Suleiman, E.N. (eds) (1980) *Presidents and Prime Ministers*, Washington, DC: American Enterprise Institute.

Rosen, B. (1981) 'Uncertainty in the senior executive service', *Public Administration Review*, 41, 2: 203–7.

Salaman, L.M. (1981) 'The presidency and domestic policy formulation', in H. Heclo and L. Salaman (eds), *The Illusion of Presidential Government*, Boulder, Colorado: Westview Press.

Salon, S. (1980) 'La politique de choix des fonctionnaires en France', in C. Debbasch (ed.), *La Fonction publique en Europe*, Paris: CNRs.

Schain, M. (1981) 'Communist control of municipal councils and urban political change', in P. Cerny and M. Schain (eds), *French Politics and Public Policy*, London: Methuen.

Scharpf, F.W. Reissert, B. and Schnabel, F. (1976) *Politikverflechtung: Theorie und Empirie des Kooperativen Föderalismus in der Bundesrepublik*, Kronberg: Scriptor.

Schattschneider, E.E. (1960) *The Semisovereign People*, New York: Holt, Rinehart & Winston.

Schick, A. (1981) 'The problem of presidential budgeting', in H. Heclo and L. Salaman (eds), *The Illusion of Presidential Government*, Boulder, Colorado: Westview Press.

Schmidt, J. (1983) 'Legal protection against public authority in the Federal Republic of Germany', *International Review of Administrative Sciences*, 49, 2: 194–209.

Schwarz, J. (1980) 'Exploring a new role: the British House of Commons in the 1970s', *American Political Science Review*, 74, 1: 23–37.

Searls, E. (1981) 'Ministerial *cabinets* and élite theory', in J. Howarth and P.G. Cerny (eds), *Élites in France*, London: Frances Pinter.

Sedgemore, B. (1980) *The Secret Constitution: an analysis of the political establishment*, London: Hodder & Stoughton.

Seidentopf, H. (1980) 'La politique de choix des fonctionnaires en Republique Fédérale d'Allemagne', in C. Debbasch (ed.), *La Fonction publique en Europe*, Paris: CNRS.

Seidman, H. (1980) *Politics, Position and Power*, 3rd edn, New York: Oxford University Press.

Selznick, P. (1958) *The TVA and the Grass Roots*, New York: Harper & Row.

Sharpe, L.J. (1976) 'Instrumental participation and urban government', in J.A.G. Griffith (ed.), *From Policy to Administration*, London: Allen & Unwin.

Shepherd, R. (1983) 'Ministers and special advisers: tilting the balance away from Cabinet', *Public Money*, 3, 3: 33–5.

Sheriff, P. (1976) 'The sociology of public bureaucracies', *Current Sociology*, 24: 1–175.

Southern, D. (1979) 'West Germany', in F. Ridley (ed.), *Government and Administration in Western Europe*, Oxford: Martin Robertson.

Stanley, D.T., Mann, D.E. and Doig, J.W. (1967) *Men Who Govern*, Washington, DC: Brookings Institution.

Study of Parliament Group (1980) 'Parliament and the economy in Great Britain', in D. Coombes and S.A. Walkland (eds), *Parliaments and Economic Affairs*, London: Heinemann.

Suleiman, E.N. (1974) *Politics, Power and Bureaucracy in France*, Princeton, NJ: Princeton University Press.

Suleiman, E.N. (1978) *Élites in French Society*, Princeton, NJ: Princeton University Press.

Sundquist, J. (1981) *The Decline and Resurgence of Congress*, Washington, DC: Brookings Institution.

Thoenig, J.-C. (1973) *L'Ère des technocrates*, Paris: Editions d'Organisation.

Thoenig, J.-C. (1978) 'State bureaucracies and local government in France', in K. Hanf and F.W. Scharpf (eds), *Interorganisational Policy-Making*, London: Sage.

Thoenig, J.-C. and Friedberg, E. (1976) 'The power of the field staff. The Case of the Ministry of Public Works, Urban Affairs and Housing in France', in A.F. Leemans and A. Dunsire (eds), *The Management of Change in Government*, The Hague: Martinus Nijhoff.

Thurber, J.A. (1981) 'The politics of the congressional budget process re-examined', in L.C. Dodd and B.I. Oppenheimer (eds), *Congress Reconsidered*, Washington, DC: Congressional Quarterly Press.

Treasury and Civil Service Committee (1983) *3rd Report. Vol. II. Minutes of Evidence. HC 236–II*, London: HMSO.

Truman, D. (1958) *The Governmental Process*, New York: Knopf.

US Advisory Commission on Intergovernmental Relations (1981a) *The Condition of Contemporary Federalism: Conflicting Theories and Collapsing Constraints. A–78*, Washington, DC: ACIR.

US Advisory Commission on Intergovernmental Relations (1981b) *An Agenda for American Federalism: Restoring Confidence and Competence. A–80*, Washington, DC: ACIR.

US Advisory Commission on Intergovernmental Relations (1981c)

The Federal Influence on State and Local Roles in the Federal System. A–89, Washington, DC: ACIR.

van Riper, P. (1983) 'The American administrative state: Wilson and the founders: an unorthodox view', *Public Administration Review*, 43, 6: 477–90.

von Beyme, K. (1983) *The Political System of the German Federal Republic*, Farnborough, Hants.: Gower.

Walker, J.L. (1983) 'The origins and maintenance of interest groups in America', *American Political Science Review*, 77, 2: 390–406.

Walkland, S.A. (1968) *The Legislative Process in Great Britain*, London: Allen & Unwin.

Weber, M. (1958) *Gesammelte Politische Schriften*, 2nd edn, Tübingen: J.C.B. Mohr.

Weber, M. (1972) *Wirtschaft und Gesellschaft*, 5th edn, Tübingen: J.C.B. Mohr.

Weller, P. (1983) 'Do prime ministers' departments really create problems?', *Public Administration*, 61, 1: 59–78.

Wildavsky, A. (1974) *The Politics of the Budgetary Process*, Boston: Little, Brown.

Wildavsky, A. (1979) 'Policy as its own cause', in A. Wildavsky (ed.) *Speaking Truth to Power. The Art and Craft of Policy Analysis*, Boston, Mass.: Little, Brown.

Wildavsky, A. (1980) *How to Limit Government Spending*, Berkeley, Cal.: University of California Press.

Wilson, F.L. (1983) 'French interest group politics: pluralist or neo-corporatist?', *American Political Science Review*, 77, 4: 895–910.

Wistrich, E. (1983) *The Politics of Transport*, London: Longman.

Wolin, S.H. (1961) *Politics and Vision*, London: Allen & Unwin.

Wolin, S.H. (1981) 'The American pluralist conception of politics', in A.L. Kaplan and D. Callahan (eds), *Ethics in Hard Times*, New York: Plenum Press.

Wolinsky, O.H. (1973) *The French Deputy*, Lexington, Mass.: Lexington Books.

Wolman, H. (1981) 'The determinants of program success and failure', *Journal of Public Policy*, 1, 4: 433–64.

Wood, R.L. (1961) *1400 Governments*, Cambridge, Mass.: Harvard University Press.

Worms, J.-P. (1966) 'Le préfet et ses notables', *Sociologie du Travail*, 3: 249–75.

Wright, D.S. (1978) *Understanding Intergovernmental Relations*, North Scituate, Mass.: Duxbury Press.

Wright, M. (1977) 'Public expenditure in Britain: the crisis of control', *Public Administration*, 55, 2: 143–70.

Wright, V. (1978) *The Government and Politics of France*, London: Hutchinson.

Wynia, B. (1974) 'Federal bureaucrats' attitudes towards a democratic ideology', *Public Administration Review*, 34, 2, 156–67.

Young, H. and Sloman, A. (1981) *No Minister*, London: British Broadcasting Corporation.

Ziller, G. (1974) *Der Bundesrat.* Düsseldorf: Droste Verlag.

Index

Adenauer, Konrad, 140
advisers, 64, 115–20, 128

Beamtenherrschaft (dominance
  by officials), 5, 9, 36–7,
  63–4, 65, 66, 106, 107, 108,
  135, 136–7, 139, 151, 166–7
Bismarck, Otto von, 12, 86, 135
Bolling Committee, 84
budgeting, 65, 66, 73–9, 114,
  128
  in Britain, 41, 44, 47, 73,
    74–5
  in France, 40, 41, 73, 75–6
  in the United States, 73,
    77–9, 138
  in West Germany, 73–76
Bundesverfassungsgericht, 122,
  126–7
bureaucracy,
  definitions of, 6–9, 167
  democracy and, 2, 10–11,
    135, 152, 162–71
  development of, 9–10,
    14–15, 165
  division of labour and, 36–7,
    42
  efficiency and, 7, 35–6
  expertise and, 9, 18, 25–6,
    28–9, 34, 108, 134, 147,
    157
  hierarchy in, 9, 36, 43–8, 53,
    63–4, 142, 145, 152

ideal type of, 5, 8–10, 14, 15,
  16, 25, 28, 38
interest groups and, 1, 11,
  91–3, 130
internal conflicts in, 37–8,
  41–2, 60, 63–4, 92, 108,
  136–7, 149, 155
judicial control and, 11, 109,
  121–7
legislatures and, 65–90
political leadership and,
  11–12, 135–9, 141, 167
power of officials in, 10–12,
  25, 132–3, 135
secrecy and, 10, 66, 82, 131
street level bureaucracy, 30,
  44–5, 131
study of, 1–3, 162–3, 171
bureaucratic politics, 165, 166,
  167–8, 170
Burnham, James, 6, 160

Cabinet, 1, 21–2, 107, 108,
  109–15
  in Britain, 104, 111–12, 113,
    115, 156
  in France, 113–14, 115, 116
  in the United States, 102,
    110–11, 114, 115
  in West Germany, 102,
    112–13, 115
cabinet (in France), 21–2, 47,
  116–17, 120, 128, 143

Carter, Jimmy, 17–18, 78
Castle, Barbara, 112, 117
civil servants,
  career structures and
    recruitment, 9, 15, 33–4,
    162
  career structures in Britain,·
    18–21, 25, 33, 118
  career structures in France,
    21–3, 25, 33, 34, 147
  career structures in the
    United States, 15–18, 24,
    25, 34
  career structures in West
    Germany, 21–5, 33–4
  educational backgrounds, 28
  length of service, 29
  political attitudes of, 27–8,
    147
  role in policy making, 30–1,
    33, 130–1, 133–4, 167
  social background, *see*
    representative
    bureaucracy
collegiality, 11, 37, 107–8, 110,
  120, 128
competences, 35, 36–8, 42–3,
  55
conflict within government
  bodies, 41–2, 92, 108, 136–7,
  149, 155
Conseil Constitutionnel, 122,
  125–6, 127
corporatism, 5, 99, 104, 154,
  156
Corps, see Grands Corps
Crosland, Anthony, 112, 141
Crossman, Richard, 20, 69–70

Dell, Edmund, 112
democracy and bureaucracy, 2,
  10–11, 135, 152, 162–71
détachement, 30, 148

Dienstwissen (knowledge of the
  service), 29, 34, 116

*École Nationale
  d'Administration*, 23, 28, 147
École Polytechnique, 22–3
educational background, 26–7,
  28
efficiency, 7, 35–6
Erhard, Ludwig, 141
expertise, 9, 10, 18, 108

federalism, *see* state and local
  government
Führerprinzip, 136
Fulton Committee, 19, 20, 28

Giscard d'Estaing, Valery, 86
Grandes Écoles, 22–3, 28, 147
Grands Corps, 22–3, 28, 30,
  147–9, 150

Haby, René, 141
Healey, Denis, 21, 117–18
Hegel, G.W.F., 2
hierarchy, 9, 35, 43–8, 53, 58,
  59, 60, 63–4, 92, 107, 142,
  145, 152

implementation, 3, 30–1, 44,
  105–6, 130–1, 140, 146, 150,
  163
incrementalism, 73–4, 79, 163,
  164
interdependence between
  government bodies, 40–3,
  55–6, 60–1, 114, 128
interest groups, 1, 11, 25, 64,
  91–106, 115, 128, 130, 132,
  134, 139–40, 145, 146, 160,
  164, 166, 167, 168
  in Britain, 57–8, 92, 103–5,

106, 112, 146, 156, 158,
163
in France, 92, 98–100, 100,
105, 106, 146, 150
in the United States, 17, 92,
94–7, 100, 105, 106, 119,
123, 124, 150, 152, 153,
160
in West Germany, 92, 100–3,
105, 106, 153, 154–5
iron triangles, 94–6, 152

Jackson, Andrew, 16
judicial review, 109, 121–2,
124, 129
in Britain, 124–5
in France, 124, 125–6, 127
in the United States, 122–4
in West Germany, 124,
126–7
Juristenmonopol (lawyers'
monopoly in
recruitment), 28

Kafka, Franz, 170

legislatures, 25, 27, 115,
121–2, 132, 145, 164, 168
as check on executive, 11,
64, 65–8, 79–80
as training ground for
leaders, 12, 67, 85, 150
in Britain, 68–9, 70, 71, 72,
73, 74–5, 80–1, 83, 85,
86–7, 145, 189, 190
in France, 67, 68–9, 70, 71,
72, 73, 75–6, 81–2, 85, 86,
89, 113, 143–4, 145
in the United States, 17, 29,
32, 67, 68, 71–3, 77–9,
83–5, 89, 93, 95, 96, 97,
119, 145, 151
in West Germany, 68–9,

70–1, 72, 73, 74–5, 76, 81,
82–3, 85, 86, 87–9, 90,
126, 150, 153, 154
local government, *see* state and
local government

Marx, Karl, 6, 27, 136
merit appointment, 16, 18, 21,
33–4
Michels, Roberto, 160
Mills, C. Wright, 160
ministers,
careers of, 85–9, 137, 142–7,
156–7
personal staffs of, 108–9,
115–20
roles of, 133–4, 156–60, 167
ministries, *see* organisational
structure
Mitterrand, François, 22, 114,
126, 140, 144
monocratic principle, 11, 36–7,
92, 107, 108, 144
Mosca, Gaetano, 169

Nietzsche, Friedrich, 136
non-negotiable policy making,
94, 97, 100, 101, 103, 104,
105, 106, 146, 153

operating ideology, 45, 133
organisational structure, 38–43,
47, 63–4, 115, 137–8, 168

Pendleton Act, 16
plum book, 17, 18, 21
policy/implementation
distinction, 3, 30–2, 133–4
policy styles, 102, 103–4, 139,
149, 154
political appointees,
in France, 21–2, 24, 25, *see*
also cabinet
in the United States, 16–18,

21, 25, 33, 151 *see also*
    plum book
  in West Germany, 23–4, 25,
    33
political leadership, 4, 11–12,
    32–3, 34, 37, 38, 64, 67, 85,
    89, 90, 91–2, 93, 108,
    135–61, 167–71
politische Beamte, *see* political
    appointees in West Germany
power, 132–3
president,
  France, 21, 113, 125, 140,
    143
  United States, 15–18, 21, 68,
    71, 72, 77, 78, 89, 96, 122,
    128, 140, 142, 153
prime minister,
  Britain, 19, 20–1, 87, 111,
    128, 140
  France, 21, 113, 125, 140,
    143
pressure groups, *see* interest
  groups
professional-bureaucratic
  complex, 2, 93, 167
public employees, 14, 49

Reagan, Ronald, 18, 78, 140,
    141
representative bureaucracy,
    26–7, 164, 165–6

satrapic conflicts
    (*Satrapenkämpfe*), 37, 38,
    63–4, 108, 137, 152, *see also*
    bureaucracy, internal
    conflicts in
Schumpeter, Joseph, 169
secrecy, 10, 66–7, 82
Senior Executive Service, 18,
    29
specialisation, 25–30, 34, 40,
    88, 108, 134, 157

spoils system, 16, 17
state and local government,
    employment in, 49
  Weberian theory and, 48, 91
  in Britain, 50–1, 57–9, 61–3,
    73, 104
  in France, 50, 51–2, 55–7,
    58, 61, 86, 140
  in the United States, 49–50,
    52–4, 61
  in West Germany, 50, 54–5,
    59–61, 102, 153, 154, 155

Thatcher, Margaret, 20–1, 117,
    140, 158
top-down policy-making, 43–8,
    168–9

United States Supreme Court,
    122–4

Weber, Max, 1, 2, 3–5, 27,
    107–8, 148, 163, 169, 170
  on collegiality, 11, 107–8,
    111, 114
  critics of Weber, 4, 30–1, 32,
    35–6
  on division of competences,
    35–8, 42
  on federalism, 48
  on hierarchy, 45
  and ideal types, 3–4, 5, 14,
    36, 38
  ideal type of bureaucracy, 5,
    8–10, 15, 16, 28, 32, 34,
    35–6, 65, 106, 135
  on interest groups, 11, 91–3,
    167
  on legislatures, 25, 27, 34,
    65–8, 73, 81, 83, 85, 87, 89
  on political leadership,
    11–12, 32–3, 34, 38, 67,
    85, 91, 93, 135–9, 144,
    146, 152, 153, 159, 161

on politics-administration
  distinction, 30, 32–3, 45,
  66, 108, 134
on power of officials, 10–12,
  25–6, 36

problems of application,
  4–5, 14–15
on specialisation, 28–9, 134
Wilson, Woodrow, 32, 133

DATE DUE

AUG 21 '88		
DEC 1 9 1986		
DEC 0 3 1986		
DE 12 '88		
JAN 0 9 1999		
APR 21 '93		
APR 19 '93		
JUL 0 1 1999		